"our last best hope"

-President John F. Kennedy

"our last best hope"

-President John F. Kennedy

◆

Why the United Nations Stumbles
and
What the United States Should Do about It

M. James Wilkinson and Alison Broinowski
Foreword by Morton Abramowitz

iUniverse, Inc.
New York Lincoln Shanghai

"our last best hope" -President John F. Kennedy
Why the United Nations Stumbles
and What the United States Should Do about It

iUniverse books may be ordered through booksellers or by contacting:

iUniverse
2021 Pine Lake Road, Suite 100
Lincoln, NE 68512
www.iuniverse.com
1-800-Authors (1-800-288-4677)

ISBN: 978-0-595-48025-8 (pbk)
ISBN: 978-0-595-60127-1 (ebk)

Printed in the United States of America

To

Ava Broinowski Thompson and Milton Theodore Wilkinson-Grant

for a safer, fairer world to grow up in

Contents

* Section headings excerpted from the Preamble of the United Nations Charter

Foreword
by Morton Abramowitz

The United Nations has been a lightning rod for criticism in the past few years: inaction on Darfur, inability to reform, the continuing farce that is the shiny new UN Human Rights Council and the Iraq oil-for-food scandal are all blights on the operation and reputation of the organization. And yet, with many of its contributions unfeted—peacekeeping across the globe, disaster relief and humanitarian responses—the UN is a unique and indispensable actor in today's more tightly-knit, troubled world.

Over sixty years ago, US President Franklin Delano Roosevelt and his wife Eleanor were driving forces behind the UN and the Universal Declaration of Human Rights. They believed that a rules-based international order was the best way to secure freedom and security for America, and for the peoples of the world. Today, in a vastly changed and interconnected world, that simple truth is even more apt. The UN as the manifestation of this belief continues to have a vital global role, even if does not live up to its founders' hopes.

Wilkinson and Broinowski, two experienced diplomats with a gift for analysis, have written a book that succinctly depicts the UN as what it is, warts and all, and offers a road-map for its revival. The authors' contention is not earth-shattering but it is correct for the US and the world: America should do more to revitalize the UN. They offer policy planks for the next administration to achieve this goal.

Americans and their leaders, preoccupied with elections and an enervating war abroad, and often under the belief we are still in a "unipolar moment," have not caught up with the radical changes in the world. The planet's political map has been transformed by seismic shifts like the rise of China and India, a resurgent Russia, petrodollar investment flows and the persistence of international terrorism. Inherently trans-national issues are of profound concern: climate change, trade liberalization and poverty reduction. Not much is heard about this in our presidential campaign; rather our candidates mostly assert that if we just get out of Iraq, we will again be the global leader.

Regrettably, the new president will find the world recalcitrant and difficult to manage. And sooner or later, he or she will face the questions: Where does the UN fit in all this? How will it help us meet our policy goals?

Our two authors argue the UN can be a more effective actor on the new world stage, and America will be well served by investing the effort to make it so. I agree.

The UN is the temple of multilateralism. The US parented the UN in 1945, but came to look upon it as something of an errant child, or worse, an absolute impediment to the achievement of important goals—a development that reached its zenith with the present administration. The Bush Administration has had little patience for the time and effort—which in any case can never be totally successful—to meld the disparate interests of 192 UN member states, especially when a substantial proportion of them seem to be congenitally anti-American and anti-Israel. The resultant perception inside the beltway that "the UN" is ineffective is unfair if one takes into account the full panoply of the organization's good works such as peacekeeping in Haiti, aiding refugees in Chad, stopping SARS and so on. But the charge rings true when it comes to big ticket items like Iraq, Kosovo and Darfur, which have tied the Security Council up in knots.

Nevertheless, there is growing realization across Washington, and indeed the country, that the Bush approach to foreign policy is dead, and the search for alternatives is well underway. The cry of multilateralism is increasingly heard in the land. While the rhetoric of multilateralism may roll off candidates' tongues, particularly Democrats, it will be a difficult policy transformation for a proud and powerful nation, whoever wins. Empowering the UN to tackle major issues such as environmental degradation, nuclear disarmament and international justice necessarily means a diminishing of US power, and arguably, even its sovereignty. In the real world, it remains to be seen whether Washington power centers, especially the US Senate, will be prepared to make the kind of concessions necessary to practice effective multilateralism.

Wilkinson and Broinowski take the issue of UN performance head on, making no bones about the organization's shortcomings. By their analysis, the member states bear the lion's share of the blame, and Washington stands out as the principal villain for systematically undermining the UN and international law through the UN-bashing days of the Reagan Administration and Senator Jesse Helms. The Clinton Administration, they find, bears heavy responsibility for Security Council failures on Bosnia, Somalia, Iraq sanctions and above all Rwanda. And under George W. Bush, the UN had little chance to get its act together with John Bolton in the job of Ambassador from the world's only superpower. The Bush Administration's anti-UN bias has left the US at odds with most of its friends around the world. It has also deprived Washington of a useful tool for advancing America's own values.

Despite the US vs. The Rest brouhahas in UN halls in recent years, Washington is still a vital part of the UN's drive train. West Europeans, the authors believe, along with Japan and to a lesser degree China and some emerging powers for reasons involving their own world standing, would all rather work with, not against, a new, more open and cooperative American presence in the UN … assuming of course that Washington has sellable policies and is willing to invest the necessary high-level attention. How much the worst instincts of third world demagogues can be reined in is more problematic.

The UN has never been the centerpiece of American foreign policy, but it once was a respected cornerstone. Is it worth the candle for America to make the UN again a pillar of its foreign policy and take on the legion of mistrustful, if not all hostile, Ambassadors seated in the General Assembly and Security Council? Wilkinson and Broinowski answer yes, and not just because they think the US can engineer some useful resolutions. They see the UN as a long underutilized means to showcase US leadership and advance the values American people want their country to stand for. Beyond that, UN leadership should also, they point out, bring concrete benefits in burden sharing, even if Washington remains deep in a hole of resentment and distrust when it comes to Afghanistan and Iraq. But the US must be realistic in measuring what it can usefully seek to do.

As America tries to deal with the consequences of its misfired Iraq expedition and the host of other challenges lurking in a murky future, this book will sharpen our thoughts on the uses and misuses of the UN and where it fits into Washington policies. The authors suggest an approach and specific policy elements that merit serious attention, even as they make clear they do not expect the UN will be any kind of panacea.

Despite Iraq, the US continues to enjoy its status as planetary king of the hill, with no competitors of equivalent might. Unfortunately that is changing. The US failed to use its "unilateral moment" to create viable new institutions or improve old ones to make itself and everyone else safer, freer, and more prosperous. It still has a waning opportunity to make the UN a more useful organization and to reform it to meet the challenges that confront us all. Dismissing the UN and failing to stand up for our principles in its governing bodies will only lead to more policy error.

Washington
September 2007

Morton Abramowitz is a senior fellow at The Century Foundation. He formerly served as President of the Carnegie Endowment for International Peace, Assistant Secretary of State, US Ambassador to Turkey, and US Ambassador to Thailand.

PART I

We the Peoples of the United Nations

1

The United Nations—"our last best hope"

○ ○

To that world assembly of sovereign states, the United Nations, our last best hope in an age where the instruments of war have far out-paced the instruments of peace, we renew our pledge of support—to prevent it from becoming merely a forum for invective—to strengthen its shield of the new and the weak—and to enlarge the area in which its writ may run.

—John F. Kennedy, Inaugural Address, January 20, 1961

Is the United Nations still the best international framework to deal with today's global challenges? The world's agenda is daunting: threats from international terrorism, WMD proliferation, pandemic disease and environmental degradation, and in parallel an equally imperative set of humanitarian issues led by poverty, human rights, political oppression, and mass displacements of populations. Looming in the background is the vast disparity between the less fortunate inhabitants of our planet and those of us who live in relative luxury, health and freedom.

There may be a better world order, but the UN is what we have. It is working day-in, day-out on the full range of global challenges. It will not be replaced or radically modified in the foreseeable future. This is a book about how governments can do much, much more with the UN system that is already in place, and why America should again put itself in the forefront of such an effort.

John F. Kennedy had faith in the potential of the UN and the vision of its principal founder, Franklin D. Roosevelt. Returning from his meeting with Churchill and Stalin at Yalta in 1945, FDR told Congress he had achieved agreement on "a common ground of peace. It spells, it ought to spell," he continued, "the end of the system of unilateral action and exclusive alliances and spheres of influence and balances of power and all the other expedients that have been tried for centuries, and have always failed. We propose to substitute for all these a universal organization in which all peace-loving nations will finally have a chance to join ..."

FDR's concept of truly universal participation opened grand new possibilities for global cooperation. It has proved to be both the genius and the curse of the United Nations. On the one hand, its 192 members drive the UN in many different directions, frequently right off the tracks and sometimes to the point of total immobilization. On the other hand, because it is global, the UN has been able to advance universal values and alleviate suffering in virtually every country on the planet; its reach has been essential to regulate commerce across borders and to curtail diseases that know no borders; and it has the scope to subsume regional security contentions in a broader framework for peace.

There is still an extraordinary opportunity for governments and the UN to expand the peace. Since the end of the Cold War, the world has enjoyed a period of relative harmony between major powers—military competition is muted, and an outbreak of war between them is almost unthinkable. There was much talk in the early 1990s of a new, more safe and stable world order, but governments were unable to seize the moment in any systematic way. The door remains open, however, and UN forums continue with occasional success to promote ideas for enhanced security, revitalized disarmament negotiations, more effective mechanisms to control crime and terrorism, and broadened acceptance of the responsibility to protect victims of brutal governments.

On the humanitarian side of the ledger, there is extraordinary need: some 25,000 people die every day from hunger or related causes; over 1,000,000 children are trafficked every year; in five countries the average person born today will not live to reach age 40; ... the chilling statistics of abject despair go on and on. In parallel, the dangers of continuing environmental degradation become more obvious with each new research report. Grappling with these facts, UN agencies, in tandem with governments, civil society, and business, have a multitude of programs under way, and they are helping millions.

But the sad fact is this: overall, the effort to make a safer, more prosperous world is falling short of what it could be. Good proposals for improvement abound—but to act on them requires global leadership.

Take me to your leader-ship!

The leader of the United Nations is the Secretary General, and many would like to see the job filled by a forceful personality who can forge consensus among cantankerous governments. In reality, however, there is no longer room at the top for someone like Dag Hammerskjold, who became a legend for his ability to personally influence outcomes and take actions without full approval from all the big powers. Today's Secretary General has to operate in a far more limited space between developing world governments that represent the majority of member states and a small number of rich governments that control most of the resources. First and foremost among the latter of course is Washington, which in 1996 denied Boutros Boutros-Ghali the traditional second term as UN Secretary General because he strayed too far off the course preferred by the US.

"In order to function, the (UN) system still cries out for far-sighted American leadership"—that was the clarion call from retiring UN Secretary General Kofi Annan in his farewell address at the Truman Library. His successor, Ban Ki-moon, made the same point less directly in his October 2006 speech accepting the position: "Only the Member States can revitalize this organization." Ban left unspoken the corollary—that only America, the one global superpower of our times, can be the engine of success in such an endeavor.

Instead of seeking to lead the UN, however, the Bush Administration has spurned it in favor of the unilateralism and exclusive alliances that FDR found so wanting. Although Washington has been happy to fund many UN humanitarian and regulatory activities, under Bush it has also actively worked to limit the organization's scope and to undermine the role of international law. Much damage has been done, and the UN's prospects for recovering lost ground hinge on November 2008, when Americans will elect a new president.

The US moved to the cusp of a new era in November 2006, when Americans remade their Congress by electing Democratic Party majorities in both Houses. The country's mood had shifted as it became clear the Bush Administration's grandiose plan to reshape the Middle East by force was failing miserably, and in the process dragging down America's aspirations to serve as a moral beacon for oppressed peoples. Polls showed that in 2006, US voters by large majorities wanted Washington to work with other countries on "shared ideas of what is best for the world as a whole," with less emphasis on military force and more on diplomacy.[1] That equates to better ties with traditional allies and greater US participation in the UN.

The US alone has the combination of economic and military power to take on the UN leadership role. The West Europeans at times aim to be out in front, but when priorities diverge across the Atlantic, even the 27 countries of the EU taken together do not have the weight to bring America along, much less to shoulder it out of the way. Newly emerging powers like China, India and Brazil seek more influence and are gaining ground rapidly, but for the next decade or so at least, they will not be able to match the US or the EU with the requisite donor dollar capacity or military power projection capability.

Close identification with the UN infused the foreign policies of Presidents Truman, Eisenhower and Kennedy. Their successors struggled to cope with the clamor from newly independent countries for economic justice and for redress from former colonizers. In the 1970's, anti-colonialism became synonymous with anti-capitalism and anti-Americanism. Moreover, the Cold War meant the major security issues of nuclear disarmament and the war in Vietnam had to be dealt with outside the Security Council's ambit. At the same time, the Nixon-Kissinger "realist" foreign policy further displaced the UN by de-emphasizing human rights in favor of short term American interests to justify dealings with dictatorships, like Pinochet's regime in Chile, Suharto in Indonesia, Argentina's Videla, the military junta in Greece and others.

In the 1980s, President Ronald Reagan's Administration rejected the Third World's invective directed at the US, walked away from the Law of the Sea negotiations and withdrew the US from compulsory jurisdiction of the International Court of Justice. Reagan's aggressive tactics opened a Pandora's Box—American conservatives exploited his policy shift to advance their more extreme objectives of downgrading the UN and curtailing international law. As we shall see in the next chapter, the influence of a reactionary America-first ethos from Reagan to George W. Bush propagated US policies that weakened the UN and further fragmented the alliance of western democracies which had kept the organization working all through the Cold War.

Washington's turn away from multilateralism has left the UN scrambling to articulate its purposes and retain its credibility in America. Although a majority of Americans still have a positive view of the UN, two decades of steady UN bashing by conservatives has accentuated a negative agenda. Allegations of scandals and recitation of errors get more than their fair share of news coverage.

An overhaul of the UN and its many parts is well past due to be sure, but member states are far from agreement on what to reform or how to do it. For better or worse, the UN will be around looking much as it does now until greater consensus can be forged. That will take years. Given this reality, governments need to focus on improving performance and programs within the existing framework while their diplomats seek ways out of the reform impasse.

Values, interests, and Washington politics

Restoring the UN to its former pride of place in American foreign policy would help the nation to reset its moral compass. At the same time, such a step is essential to reenergize the UN. Some of the most sensible advice for the next US President has come from those who argue for a US return to a "value-based" foreign policy, including respect for international law, and for promotion of new coalitions within—not instead of—the UN.[2] The values in question are those which America articulated to guide its government and society. They are also universal.

Universal values are what the UN is all about. Americans played leading roles to write the UN Charter, the Universal Declaration of Human Rights, the Convention against Genocide and other seminal documents. They did not intend to put down mere words, but to initiate a process that would set standards and over time require compliance. Much remains to be done to answer "humankind's cry for help," a cry that is in Yale historian Paul Kennedy's words, the "strongest argument for the continued validity and empowerment of the United Nations."[3]

Then too, there are strong practical arguments for greater US engagement with the UN. Timothy Wirth, President of the UN Foundation, in testimony before Congress in February 2007, spoke to the concerns of the many Washington politicians who focus squarely on cost-benefit returns to tax-payers. "The rationale for global partnerships and working through the United Nations," he said, "are threefold: burden-sharing, effectiveness and (America's) reputation."[4] Wirth highlighted both the need for global approaches and the leverage of implementation where others contribute not only funds, but also, for example, military personnel and doctors, or improve laws to intercept funds headed for terrorist organizations. We shall return to these themes in the central sections of this book.

Leading lights of the centrist or liberal American establishment urge re-energizing the transatlantic alliance, but some, notably former National Security Advisor Zbigniew Brzezinski in his recent book, *Second Chance,* have made only passing reference to the UN. Richard Haass, President of the non-governmental Council on Foreign Relations, went further in *The Opportunity*, his call for multilateral integration, when he wrote that America "should not avoid the UN Security Council," although he found "it and the UN a too brittle and too narrow instrument to be centerpiece of any attempt at this moment to build a more integrated world."[5]

But to leave the UN on some back-burner forgoes valuable opportunities to exert global influence. And in any case, reinvigorating US-European ties implies harmonizing American policies with the high priority that Europeans accord to the UN. When Washington did invest in the UN under the first President Bush, the effort paid off handsomely: the Security Council supported the use of force to free Kuwait from Iraqi aggression, and other countries contributed over $50 billion to cover most of the cost of US military action in the 1990/91 Gulf War that followed. Later in the elder Bush's Administration, the US was able to engineer repeal of the infamous 1975 General Assembly "Zionism is racism" resolution. These American successes were achieved by leadership, diplomatic skill and hard work. They can be replicated.

America can lead, but cannot by itself make the UN significantly more effective. There is too much to be done across the range of security, development and human rights problems. Western Europe, Japan, New Zealand, Australia and Canada must join with the US to define realistic goals and agree on the means to achieve them. Russia, China and India must contribute more substantially and less selfishly to UN work. Ways must be found to reassure nations caught up in the vexing difficulties of the Middle East, and to ameliorate the problems of governments beset by corruption and incompetence. These are tall orders, but an American President who embraces multilateral approaches in good faith will find willing partners.

This book

Against the background of profound change in the making at home and abroad, this book pulls together the current threads of discussion about the UN and its future. We hope to shed light for the general reader on what the most important issues are, how to assess the UN realistically, and most importantly how to understand the crucial role of UN member states, in particular the US. Above all, we shall try to lay out a viable program of action—what America can and should do to better realize the enormous potential of the UN.

Our perspective is that of practitioners who have seen the UN up close, warts and all. We both worked at our Missions to the UN (for the US and Australia, respectively) in New York in 1989/1990 during those heady days when the Cold War came to its welcome end, and much was made of the wonderfully promising possibilities for the new era to come. We later watched with dismay as the prospect of a better world order failed to materialize. Why this happened and what can yet be done are questions central to this book.

We start by examining the deep cracks in the foundations of UN support. There are many, of which the North-South divide has proved the most enduring. The once vast East-West canyon supposedly disappeared with the end of the Cold War, but Russia and China still find reason to line up against the US, UK and France in the Security Council. Arguably, the most damaging divide in the present UN context is now that between America and most of the other nations with governments rooted in western democratic traditions. It makes little sense that America should repeatedly isolate itself from its natural allies, but that is in fact the case, and it is robbing the UN of its capabilities.

We then take up the fundamental tension between national interests and the global good. The world public favors greater use of the UN, and most political leaders ceremonially extol its virtues, but when it comes to votes in UN forums, many governments still put short-term gain ahead of far-sighted investment that would strengthen the ability of UN institutions to advance the Charter's goals. Is the UN as conceived in 1945 still able to meet the needs of our rapidly changing world?—yes, if member states act more unselfishly to give it the right kind of support.

But devils always lurk in the details. Our central chapters, updating the analysis of our previous work (*The Third Try: can the UN work?*[6]), examine the state of affairs in the three main areas of the UN Charter's mandate—ending the scourge of war; affirming faith in fundamental human rights, and promoting social progress and better standards of life. What is working, what isn't and why not? Why hasn't the world collectively done better, given the technological advances of recent years and the great wealth amassed by developed countries? And what can the UN do to coordinate or amplify the contributions of non-governmental organizations (NGOs), mega-philanthropists, corporations and politicized religion, which are all playing ever-more influential roles in our ever-more interconnected world?

Our concluding sections set forth what has to happen to revitalize the UN. The obvious starting point is America and the policies it must adopt to reassert leadership in the international community. A number of measures are self-evident, such as acceding to treaties already signed and working with others instead of insisting on made-in-America approaches. But change has to go deep to be effective and lasting, and in our last chapter, we propose eight foreign policy planks to advance American goals through the UN system and help restore American credibility around the world.

2

UN Member States—Global House Divided

○ ○

One would like to believe that our joint efforts to put an end to the era of wars, confrontation and regional conflicts, aggression against nature, the terror of hunger and poverty, as well as political terrorism, will be comparable with our hopes. This is our common goal, and it is only by acting together that we may attain it.

—Mikhail Gorbachev, UN General Assembly Address, December 7, 1988

The United Nations does a great deal of good work. Almost everyone finds reason to praise frontline agencies like the World Health Organization (WHO) for combating global health threats, the International Civil Aviation Organization (ICAO) for regulating air traffic, UNICEF for helping children, UNHCR for saving refugees, and UN teams for providing disaster relief. Although sometimes less warmly commended, UN organizations for peacekeeping, economic development, human rights and environmental protection have also had considerable success. It must be said, however, that the UN record is peppered with scandals and errors, and a long list of goals is yet to be reached, especially in Africa and on human rights.

The UN could surely do better on all fronts, but twenty five years after the end of the Cold War, the organization is still a house divided against itself. And divided, UN member states are failing to deal effectively with the world's most critical problems.

Why is the UN so fractious? What are the implications of the gulf between the rich North and the poor South, and can it be narrowed anytime soon? Why do so many Third World countries embrace anti-American rhetoric at the UN, and give pariah states membership on human rights bodies, and sometimes even on the Security Council? Why does America so often go its own way, rejecting compromise even with its fellow democracies?

In this chapter, we explore these questions. The answers have important implications for the multilateral leadership role Americans hope their country will play under their next President.

Multilateralism and its difficulties

In 1945, Americans drew on their traditions to give the UN features of a pluralistic democratic organization. Thus, all member states, large or small, participate with one vote each in the UN General Assembly, and that body has the power of the purse. To deal with the realities of the time, however, it was necessary to give the victors of WW II extra means to protect their interests, so the Permanent Five members of the Security Council have the veto power and the Council itself has exceptional authority. The result, to paraphrase Churchill, has turned out to be the worst form of governance—except for the alternatives, which remain unacceptable to the members. No consensus has yet formed on how to make the UNGA more effective or the Security Council more democratic.

Differences are inevitable between 192 member states with disparate goals, and formation of interest groups is the stuff and substance of democratic governing bodies. Ideology cleaved the UN into the Cold War camps of East and West before the ink dried on the Charter, and two decades later, the clash of economic interests produced the on-going contentious divide between the poorer developing countries (still also called the Third World) which lie mostly in the South and the wealthier nations of the North. The Cold War ended with the collapse of Soviet communism, while the North-South divide continues as a dominant factor shaping the UN agenda.

For the UN's general health and performance today, however, the most serious division is the split between America and its traditional allies. Greater unity among the western democracies, including Japan and Korea, is critical to reduce poverty, advance justice, protect the environment, manage tensions between major powers, and make progress on the plethora of intractable regional or subregional confrontations, in particular the intense gulf between supporters of Palestinians and those of Israelis. These central challenges cannot be effectively addressed unless America rejoins the UN team it left, not in 2000 or 2003 as most seem to think, but in the early 1980's.

Understanding bloc politics—the complex and fluid alliances between groups of member states based on shared interests—holds the key to success in the UN. Every set of issues has its own dynamic, depending on the particular stakeholders, history and place on the agenda of the day. The UN is a demanding parliamentary venue, where rhetoric regularly obscures true motivations, interests change, and blocs are seldom as monolithic as they look. The next sections of this chapter examine the principal groupings and fault lines that affect outcomes in today's UN.

America—the leader's about face

For three decades after World War II, America led a coalition that provided the authority, energy, and resources to assure the UN would establish itself and function as a respected global entity. The governments of the US, West European countries, Canada, Australia, and New Zealand shaped the UN system in its present form and put up the money—in 1951, for example, they paid 67.92% of the UN's costs even before Germany and Japan began contributing. In some ways, the most striking aspect of the Cold War was not Soviet obstructionism, but the West's ability to develop the UN's global role in the face of Russian "nyets."

Impelled by a US-led axis of good, the UN grew into an imposing presence on the world stage. Early western initiatives of lasting import included adoption of the Universal Declaration of Human Rights drafted under the guiding hand of Eleanor Roosevelt, passage of the Convention on Genocide, and establishment of the Atomic Energy Commission. A long list of accomplishments followed: peacekeeping mitigated local conflicts; treaties limited the spread of nuclear weapons; international law developed new norms to regulate affairs between states; frameworks unfolded for the advocacy of human rights and environmental protection; and UN agencies eliminated smallpox, sheltered millions of refugees, helped desperate victims of natural disasters, and promoted stable economic conditions for trade and investment.

American commitment flagged, however, in the 1970's, when the host of newly independent nations flexed their voting muscle in the General Assembly. They had many legitimate bones to pick, especially the ongoing discriminatory terms of trade and commerce that impeded their development. But the validity of their case was obscured by their own political rhetoric—always passionate, not always relevant, and all too often simply outrageous. Frustrated by their relative impotence within the UN system and egged on by demagogic leaders as well as the Soviet Union, Third World representatives regularly showered abuse on the West and promoted wasteful spending to impress constituents back home. Many western governments were sympathetic in principle and therefore hesitated to confront their poorer cousins—and in any case found themselves outvoted.

American wavering became a fundamental turn away from the UN under President Ronald Reagan following his election in 1980. The most conspicuous early manifestation of the new approach was his antagonistic rejection of Third World criticism—his outspoken UN Ambassador, Jeanne Kirkpatrick, called for an end to what she termed the "preemptive capitulation" of western representatives in UN bodies. The Administration and sympathizers in Congress soon moved from words to action when the US withdrew from UNESCO and began withholding UN dues to block what it considered excessive or unreasonable expenditures.

The Reagan Administration's quarrel with the UN system went much deeper than pique over Third World invective and wasteful spending. Washington quit the Law of the Sea negotiations because the Reagan Administration's deep ideological distrust of supra-national bodies made it unwilling to accept compromise on seabed mining provisions. It was the first time America walked away from an important global negotiation rather than staying the course to hammer out a resolution. For similar ideological reasons, Reagan's Washington withdrew from compulsory jurisdiction of the International Court of Justice (ICJ), anticipating a verdict against the US for mining Nicaraguan harbors in peacetime. America has yet to rejoin the ICJ. Taken together, as Rosemary Righter correctly observed, the Reagan policies of "insistence on reasserting US power and moral eminence at the UN ... represented the radicalization of traditional US policy."[7]

Republican neocons and archconservatives, led in Congress through the 1990s on foreign policy issues by the powerful Senator Jesse Helms, exploited Reagan's legacy to spurn international law and downgrade the UN system. Their ideology—termed by scholars "American exceptionalism" or less often, "new sovereigntism"[8]—holds that the US should "pick and choose" its international arrangements and has no obligation to any higher legal authority. During his single term from 1989 to 1992, President George H.W. Bush tempered their influence and gave priority to multilateral relations. The succeeding Administration under President Clinton talked of "assertive multilateralism," but its gross errors in Somalia and Rwanda, its inability to manage the sanctions against Iraq, and the UN bashing by Republicans in Congress all threw it on the defensive. Helms held sway and the US Senate thumbed its nose at the international community, rejecting the Kyoto Protocol, the Comprehensive Test Ban Treaty, the Convention on the Rights of the Child, the Convention to Eliminate All Forms of Discrimination Against Women, the International Criminal Court, and other important cooperative endeavors. Most of America's traditional allies appealed for greater flexibility and common sense—to no avail.

The US vs. The Rest

The election of President George W. Bush in 2000 put neoconservatives firmly in control and drove more wedges between Washington and other UN members. The US chipped away at the Millennium Development Goals, petulantly insisted that the newly established Global Fund to Fight Aids, Tuberculosis and Malaria operate outside the UN system, obstructed talks on global warming, and in effect scuttled nuclear arms negotiations. After the attacks of September 11, 2001, ideology trumped common sense, when Washington showed little interest in mobilizing a broad coalition or utilizing the Security Council to take advantage of the world-wide outpouring of sympathy for America. Brushing aside not only the Security Council, but also NATO, the Bush Administration declared "war on terror" and relied on a small circle of allies for its military operations against the Taliban and Osama bin Laden in Afghanistan.

Then US action against Iraq dissipated good will from 9/11 and widened old rifts. In March 2003, Bush strained US-European relations to the breaking point when he ordered the invasion after dismissing the (well-founded) objections of several EU governments and declaring the Security Council "irrelevant" for not endorsing the US position. The United Kingdom and, on a smaller scale, Australia joined the US with significant combat forces. Poland and Denmark contributed some troops, and 46 other nations expressed support. The US could thus claim 50 nations in its "coalition of the willing," but except for the UK, the input of the others was token at best and miniscule in comparison to contributions given the US for the Iraq-Kuwait military operations of 1990–91.

European hesitance over Iraq infuriated neocons who had long belittled Europe (except the UK) as feckless and weak for failing to maintain a stronger military and, worse, for disagreeing with Washington's security strategies. "It is time to stop pretending that Europeans and Americans share a common view of the world, or even that they occupy the same world," wrote American conservative Robert Kagan on the eve of the American invasion of Iraq.[9] Although Kagan's formulations strike many on both sides of the Atlantic as absurd, distrust of Europe not only runs deep in American right wing circles, but also enjoys recurrent media exposure and exerts disproportionately strong influence in the US Congress.

Differences over the nature of an ideal international system lie at the center of the transatlantic rift. From intellectual conviction as well as their own experience, Europeans (and Japanese) believe that today's most pressing global problems require multilateral solutions. They are at best puzzled, more often shocked, when they see Washington putting more faith in military operations than diplomacy. The reactionary, go-it-alone record of recent American diplomacy goes very deep—well beyond the highly publicized bones of contention like the Kyoto Protocol and the International Criminal Court. For example, in a December 2006 General Assembly vote to begin negotiation on a treaty to regulate small arms trade, 153 countries voted in favor, 24 abstained and only the US voted no. More to the point perhaps, over the years, allies have compromised with new language to accommodate US concerns on agreements covering the Law of the Sea and the Rights of the Child, but Senate conservatives then shifted ground and still refused to ratify the basic treaties.

Disturbing as they are, US-EU disagreements over foreign and security policies have to be kept in perspective. In the bigger picture, the underlying bonds between America and Europe are literally unbreakable: history and culture (the 2000 US census counted 172 million European-Americans), economic connections (annual two-way flow of goods, services and direct investment is about $1 trillion), and shared approaches to a range of security issues (NATO, anti-terrorist programs, numerous peacekeeping operations, and sometimes, even Arab-Israeli peace initiatives). From their side, Europeans follow American politics closely, understand the depth of current domestic opposition to the Bush Administration, and would welcome a more centrist government in Washington with open arms.

Nonetheless, the two populations have pursued different tracks on some very basic issues such as social programs and the role of religion in public life. The question is whether they will also go their separate ways on notions of global governance. The difficulty of restoring cooperation in this area should not be underestimated. Even if the next Administration attunes itself more closely to Europe and Democratic Party majorities continue in the Congress, the American system is such that a relatively small number of conservative legislators can block ratifications of international treaties and funding of UN programs.

The Great Divide—South vs. North

The American right wing and even some liberals view the two main political coalitions of the Third World—the Non-Aligned Movement (NAM) and the Group of 77 (G-77)[10]—as virtual enemies. The support both organizations have given to Palestinians is equated with aid to terrorism; their resistance to UN reform comes across as irresponsible; their fight for a greater voice in economic aid flows is seen as cover for poor governance and corruption at home; their performance in UN human rights forums is taken as protection for brutal dictatorships. NAM and G-77 representatives strike back at such criticisms with their own litany of charges against the wealthy countries of the North for thinly disguised imperialism, exploitation of globalization to serve big corporations, and a mean-spirited unwillingness to give the South either reasonable prices for its products or a fair share of global resources. There is, in short, a dialogue of the deaf.

The fact is, however, that the South is not as unreasonable as many in the North believe, nor as monolithic as the NAM and G-77 would claim. In any case, the North still holds most of the cards, and it is neither wise nor necessary for Washington leaders to dismiss 130 governments as if they were errant schoolboys. Progress on addressing the South's very real economic grievances will come not from confrontation, but from good-faith dialogue and cooperation. To set the stage for our later discussion of how best to approach these difficult tasks, the following paragraphs recap what drives the NAM and G-77, and how they operate today.

The divide between rich and poor countries surged to the fore in the late 1950's. It reflected the harsh realities of poverty in less fortunate nations, then as now mostly south of the equator, and the gross economic disparity between them and the industrialized countries in the North. The post-colonial influx of new UN members, primarily underdeveloped countries struggling with weak political and economic systems, transformed the General Assembly from a solidly pro-US forum into a platform for Third World activism. The initial political organizing was relatively benign and stemmed in large part from a sensible desire to steer a safe path between the two protagonists of the Cold War. To this end, 29 governments met in Bandung, Indonesia in 1955, and issued an unexceptional ten-point declaration to foster their continued cooperation based on the UN Charter and the Five Principles championed by Indian Prime Minister Jawarhalal Nehru.

The mood of the South, however, soon turned combative. Economic stagnation, corruption, social inequities and incompetent governance were shattering dreams of rapid post-independence progress. The blame in the eyes of the South lay squarely on the doorsteps of the former ruling powers, which in fact had generally exploited their colonies for raw materials and failed to prepare them for independence. The South's discontent expressed itself through three main vehicles: the NAM with heavily political overtones, the G-77 with a stronger spotlight on economic issues, and UNCTAD (the Conference on Trade and Development) which started as a meeting and morphed into a permanent think tank intended to help the Third World.

The NAM was founded in 1964 by the 47 governments that participated in the Second Conference of Non-Aligned Heads of State in Cairo. (The first such summit had taken place in Belgrade in 1961 at the invitation of President Tito.) The early NAM was dominated by strong personalities such as Yugoslavia's Tito, Cuba's Castro and Zambia's Kaunda. The group found common cause on many UN agenda items, including unwavering opposition to apartheid in South Africa and rock-solid support for the Palestinians against Israel. By 1970, it lost considerable credibility in the West, owing to the close cooperation—in fact, alignment—with the Soviet Union displayed by Castro and others, but it stayed together and even survived a major internal split over the 1979 Soviet invasion of Afghanistan, when Muslim members parted ways with the pro-Moscow contingent.

UNCTAD was first convened as a multilateral conference in 1964 to take up the economic grievances of developing countries. Contentious from the start, UNCTAD was transformed at Third World insistence from a one-time conference to a permanent UN organization—with a Secretariat and meetings every four years—for research, debate, policy initiatives and technical assistance for developing countries. Initially, its efforts to obtain better terms of trade and finance for its clients met with some success, as did its campaign against excesses of trans-national corporations. However, the 1973 "oil shock" and the South's ill-advised proposals to radically "reform" the world economy and control international media provoked a backlash from the North, led by the US, which sharply reduced UNCTAD's resources and influence.

The G-77, the strongest voice of the South today, retains its original name, although it now numbers 130 governments. It sprang to life on the margins of UNCTAD I in 1964, when seventy-seven developing nations joined forces "to articulate and promote their collective economic interests and enhance their joint negotiating capacity ... and promote South-South cooperation."[11] Since then it has aggressively pushed the South's economic and social agenda in the General Assembly, ECOSOC, UNCTAD and specialized UN agencies. Driven by the South's perceptions of economic injustice and using its substantial majority, the G-77 demanded a "right to development," transfers of resources from North to South, establishment of commodity producer cartels, and a range of measures to give developing country governments more influence over trade, investment and information flows. In the 1970s, the G-77 proposed a New International Economic Order and a bit later a New World Information and Communication Order, both of which may have had some justification, but wildly over-reached and became little more than declaratory posturing. Since those low-water marks, the G-77 has moderated its approach, while still holding governments of the North accountable for economic exploitation.

The gap between the well-being of people in developed compared to those in developing countries remains obscenely real by any measurement and will continue to generate tension between North and South. While experts argue over who or what is ultimately to blame, upwards of three billion people in the South remain mired in abject poverty, caught between poor governance at home and tight purse strings in the countries that could do more to help. Developing country solidarity remains a powerful force in the UN, where declaratory policies count for a great deal, and small countries find their only opportunity to voice their grievances before an international audience. The developing countries steadfastly resist many of the North's UN reform proposals, fearing loss of the influence they enjoy by virtue of majorities in the General Assembly and in bodies such as the Human Rights Council.

The G-77 with its 130 members and the NAM with 112 retain a strong political base as of 2007. The G-77 is well-organized with annual ministerial meetings, summit conclaves every five years, and permanent Chapter offices in cities where international organizations have a major presence. It leads the South's charge for more aid from developed countries along with more say over how it is used. The G-77 has become somewhat less political than the NAM, but the communiqué from its 2006 ministerial meeting still concluded with a ritualistic condemnation of Israel.

The NAM has a less formal structure and operates by consensus primarily through working groups, the most important of which is its Security Council Caucus. When it sticks together, this Caucus can wield a de facto veto since it often holds seven Security Council seats (from among the three Africans, two Latin Americans, two Asian and one East European places), enough to block the nine vote majority needed for passage of a Security Council resolution. The NAM still serves, though not exclusively, as a sounding board for radicals, and its 2006 Summit in Havana featured speeches by Fidel Castro (recorded, since Castro himself was too ill to be present), Venezuela's Hugo Chavez and a representative from North Korea.

The third major standing caucus of the South is the G-24, comprising two dozen of the larger southern economies plus China as a special observer. Its 2007 agenda concentrates on increasing aid and investment flows, and reducing what it sees as the "democratic deficit" from under-representation on World Bank and International Monetary Fund governing bodies. The G-24's major meetings are held twice a year at the ministerial level to coordinate lobbying actions just before World Bank and IMF sessions. More conservative and focused than the NAM or the G-77, the G-24 includes economic powerhouses India and Brazil, along with Mexico, which dropped out of the G-77 after concluding its free trade agreement with the US.

Finally, and perhaps an indicator of better things to come, are the two G-20s. The elder G-20, formed in 1999, represents the world's largest industrial economies, composed of the seven biggest individual countries, plus the EU, China, India, Brazil, South Africa, Saudi Arabia, Turkey and others. The finance ministers and central bank governors of this G-20 work together to promote "high and sustainable growth" of the global economy. The other G-20, dating from 2003, is led by the same developing countries and concerns itself primarily with reducing the agricultural subsidies of industrialized countries. This G-20 includes China,

Brazil, India, Cuba and other countries with substantial agricultural sectors. In 2007, representatives of India and Brazil on behalf of the G-20 met with counterparts from the US and EU in an unsuccessful effort to resuscitate the important Doha round of international trade talks. Both G-20s, whether or not they produce agreements on any given issue, facilitate serious and substantive communication on economic issues between North and South, largely shorn of the political diatribes that have so often taken the G-77 and NAM down blind alleys.

While the South can periodically muster an imposing unity, especially on its gut economic issues as well as the Palestinian question, the G-77 and NAM are rife with internal contradictions. The rise of OPEC and energy prices split the South into oil haves and have-nots. More generally, it is hard to define much common ground between G-77 countries like Singapore (US $27, 400 GNI per capita in 2005) and Cyprus ($16,500) on the one hand, and those like Burundi ($100) and Liberia ($130) on the other. Nonetheless, governments find the appearance of large group solidarity politically useful, and the more clever (or more duplicitous) have their cake and eat it too by posturing at the UN while doing important business elsewhere. An old game perhaps, but often played well and successfully.

Regional groups—my neighbor right or wrong

Like people, countries also identify with their neighbors and the special interests of their neighborhood. Recognizing this, the UN Charter specified that the non-permanent members of the Security Council should be selected with "due regard" not only to the member's contribution to the purposes of the UN, but also "to equitable geographical distribution." This principle of allotting seats by a geographic formula became firmly entrenched, and today elections to the Security Council, the Human Rights Council and almost every other UN body are structured by dividing the number of open seats among five geographic groups. Thus, for example, of the ten non-permanent Security Council seats, three are filled by African states, two from Latin America, two from Western Europe, two from Asia, and one from Eastern Europe.

The groups are:

> **Western European and Others Group (WEOG)**: 27 members including western Europeans, Australia, Canada, New Zealand and Turkey. Israel participates in WEOG for activities at the UN in New York, a limited membership but one that allowed an Israeli to be elected Vice-President of the

General Assembly in 2005. The US is technically not a member but partici-pates for elections to seats on numerous US bodies.

Eastern European Group: 23 members including Russia and the former states of the Soviet Union, along with the states of the former Yugoslavia.

Latin American and Caribbean Group (GRULAC): 33 members.

African Group: 53 members.

Asian Group: 53 members, including Japan and other East Asian states, Oceania, South Asia and the Middle East.

UN voting procedures allow only the regional groups to nominate candidates for their allocated seats, and the General Assembly then votes as a whole on the names submitted. This applies not only to memberships, but also to officer posi-tions, e.g., president or vice-president, which for large entities like the General Assembly and major world conferences are similarly apportioned by region. Typ-ically, the regional caucus will propose just enough nominees to fill the open seats, thereby assuring the election of its choice. Each group also tends to rotate nominees so that all the countries within the group, even the small ones and the rogues, eventually get a term on important bodies—as in 2007 when the African Group nominated Burkina Faso and Libya for its two open slots on the Security Council.

The process regularly puts pariah states on UN bodies. In the case of the Human Rights Council particularly, regional group nominations have undermined the purpose and effectiveness of the body itself by repeatedly filling seats with unde-serving candidates that qualify only by virtue of belonging to the geographic group. Vote trading, even vote buying, can play a role in any given election, but many countries in Africa and Asia simply find their interests better served by upholding group loyalty rather than tilting toward the kind of activism favored by western democracies and NGOs. Among other considerations, it has provided a safe way for some of them to forestall potentially uncomfortable questions about their own practices. Such sensitivity is not unique to developing coun-tries—even the US and Australia have bristled and rejected reports from UN Spe-cial Rapporteurs criticizing laws or treatment of indigenous populations.

From time to time, a regional group will split and nominate more candidates than open seats, thereby allowing the General Assembly vote to decide the out-come. Washington in 2006 took advantage of this possibility to keep Venezuela off the Security Council by lobbying GRULAC to nominate Guatemala as a competitor for the open seat, which led to deadlock in the General Assembly until Panama slipped in as a compromise. In 2001, the US itself was ousted from the Human Rights Commission by the Assembly vote when the western Europeans nominated four states for three seats—in this manner, the Europeans at the time signaled their great unhappiness with Bush Administration policies, including opposition to the Kyoto Protocol, the International Criminal Court, and a program to make AIDS medicines more available to all. The following year, the US muscled its way back onto the Commission by persuading Italy and Spain to withdraw their candidacies, leaving only enough WEOG nominees with the US included to fill the group's allocation.

Can the system be changed? Not easily and not with the confrontational approach that has dominated recent attempts to do so. It will help to "name and shame" democratic governments that take the expedient way out by suppressing their objections, but that will not be enough. Western democracies need to find the right incentives—or if need be, mix of carrots and sticks—to influence regional group governments who now find they have more to gain by being good neighbors than by "kow-towing" to outsiders.

Changing landscapes—BRICs on the move

Looking ahead, what is in store as China, Russia, India and Brazil steadily accrue more economic power and political influence? The economies of the four (BRICs, they are collectively known by their initials) are moving ahead at warp speeds and in 40 years or so could grow to equal the sum total of today's six biggest economies. South Africa, Mexico; and the South East Asia economic bloc (ASEAN) are on their heels. The growth of these economic centers and their new multinational corporations has major implications for world markets, competition for energy and mineral resources, capital flows, and development of information technology services. Lurking in the background is the question of whether the newly accrued wealth will be translated into increased military power, particularly with reference to China, if only because it has the least democratic government of the four.

New cracks and fissures have already appeared on the UN landscape. In the Security Council, China and Russia are far from being close allies, but they have expressed similar concerns over the readiness of western countries to seek intervention against human rights abuses, as manifested by the Russian veto in the case of Kosovo and the Chinese demands to tread more softly on Darfur and Myanmar. Both Moscow and Beijing have also diverged at times from western consensus positions on how to deal with the nuclear ambitions of Iran. In the economic sphere, China, India and Brazil have lined up with G-77 friends to press for changes in IMF voting procedures and for new regional trade arrangements. Success on either track would diminish powers now enjoyed by wealthy nations. Australian scholar Coral Bell, for one, anticipates a post-hegemonic world with the US facing a 'concert of powers' that, in a narrow form, may include the states denied permanent Security Council membership—India, Japan, and Germany—and in a broader form, she thinks, could be shaped by the aspirations of Mexico, Brazil, Argentina, Indonesia, Nigeria, South Africa and others.[12]

Finally, the American "war on terror" has also given rise to apprehension that there really could be a "clash of civilizations" between Muslims on the one hand and the Christian world on the other. The hard-line Bush Administration defense of Israel-right-or-wrong, the US treatment of Muslim prisoners, and its zealous hunt for Islamic terrorist suspects have all reinforced perceptions abroad that America is anti-Arab and anti-Muslim. Problems of immigration and assimilation in Europe have contributed to global uncertainty. The UN has taken some useful initiatives to encourage global dialogue between religions, but much more will have to be done to bridge gaps in understanding.

The first step to better managing the plethora of contesting interests at the UN is improved cooperation between the US and its traditional allies. America, the EU and Japan share the values that underpin the UN Charter, and they pay the bills—nearly 80% of the UN's regular budget between them. Along with their influential "medium power" colleagues—Canada, Norway, New Zealand, and Australia—they would be a potent force if they had the political will to put Charter goals above national interests and hammer out cooperative approaches in the UN.

Renewed western unity will not, however, be a panacea. The South's grievances have deep roots, and the on-rush of religious fundamentalism has yet to be fully understood. In many UN situations, the West will bump up against perceptions that the wealthy nations seek only to establish a stronger hegemony to protect their interests. Some of this will be knee-jerk reactions from ambitious demagogues, but there will also be more reasonable concerns drawn from a history of misunderstandings and Northern assurances that failed to produce expected results. A newly united West would have to be patient and flexible to avoid a monolithic arrogance that would cause more harm than good.

Progress will necessarily be slow and painful. We know how *not* to go about it. James Traub's biography of Kofi Annan paints a revealing picture of America's "trigger-happy" Ambassador, John Bolton, figuratively holding the tiller while the boat with negotiators heads over the falls to crash on the rocks. Bolton's obduracy deformed the 2005 UN Summit Declaration and diminished chances for success on restructuring the Human Rights Commission. The replacement of Bolton in late 2006 by Zalmay Khalilzad, who transferred from his posting as America's Ambassador to Iraq, heralded a more moderate Washington approach, but no fundamental change in policy.

"There are many UNs," as Kofi Annan observed after his farewell lunch with Security Council Ambassadors. He was describing the complex interplay between UN offices and member states in the case of Darfur. Indeed, big issues on the level of armed intervention, nation building, climate change, genocide, rights of women and children, terrorism, and cataclysmic disaster relief all have different constituencies, stakeholders and power brokers contending within the UN. The middle sections of this book examine how these dynamics play out on security, human rights, and development questions, the major areas of the UN's Charter mandate. The next chapter takes up a problem common to them all—how to match the vision with reality and overcome selfish national interests.

3

UN Goals—Global Vision vs. National Priorities

"The (United Nations) had the misfortune to be born with a grossly inflated vision of its interventionist power. Yet if expectations are reduced it might still be possible to reach a positive balance between vision and reality.... With all its imperfections, the United Nations is still the main incarnation of the global spirit. It alone seeks to present a vision of humankind in its organic unity."

—*Israeli Statesman Abba Eban, 1995*[13]

"No organization in the world embodies as many dreams, yet delivers as many frustrations as the United Nations," observed Gareth Evans, President of the International Crisis Group, in 2005.[14] This gap between what the world believes the UN should do and what it seems able to accomplish creates enormous problems for the organization. Governments blame the UN for their own shortcomings in tackling global problems, and finger-point at each other for not fixing the UN to make it work better. All this blocks progress on needed reforms and undermines backing for the UN. The public is left confused and dismayed.

Judging by polls, the majority of ordinary people instinctively see the UN and global cooperation as a good thing. Most governments, even those of liberal persuasion, however, focus on short-term gain to impress domestic constituencies. Political leaders, therefore, try to have their cake and eat it too by asserting support for the UN even as they pursue narrow national objectives at the expense of the global good. The UN gets caught in the middle.

This chapter examines how the visions of the UN Charter still clash with the realities of national politics, and what is needed to bridge the gap.

National interests vs. the global good

A former British Ambassador to the UN, Lord Caradon, once remarked, "There is nothing essentially wrong with the UN—except the Member States."[15] An oversimplification to be sure, but it puts the horse correctly before the cart. There should be no doubt that the starting points for change are member state votes. Governments vote on actions, pay the bills and give marching orders to the UN, not the other way around. The Secretary General can propose, but the member states dispose.

The inability of the UN to deal decisively with Darfur presents a classic illustration of national interests taking precedence over higher principle. By any reasonable assessment the government in Khartoum has committed crimes against humanity—most would say genocide—and the rest of the world has a duty to protect the victims. Washington after initial waffling declared there was genocide underway, but it has declined to take strong action that might jeopardize its tacit counter-terrorism cooperation with Khartoum or adversely affect other US objectives in the area. The West Europeans have talked tougher, but won't go it alone against Khartoum. Many Islamic governments have sided with their co-religionists in Khartoum rather than assisting those who are victims in Darfur. Beijing and Moscow have kept the brakes on in the Security Council—China has an important stake in Sudanese oil; Russia makes money from arms sales to Khartoum; and both have qualms about the precedent of UN-sponsored outside intervention in the country. Even countries like South Africa and India have been unwilling to make meaningful demands of Sudan through the Human Rights Council. In sum, all the key players have found selfish reason not to intervene even as killing and suffering continue virtually in front of their eyes.

More generally, the bigger military and economic powers, above all the US, can have it both ways on international security issues. They engage the UN when it suits them or detour around it otherwise. The five permanent members (often called "the Perm-5") of the Security Council can of course use their veto power to block any Security Council opposition to their own preferred course, but veto or not, decisive use of force by the Council is unlikely these days except in the most egregious circumstances—like Iraq's invasion of Kuwait in 1990. Thus, NATO can bomb Serbia, Israel can make military incursions into Lebanon, Ethiopia (with US backing) can intervene in Somalia, and Turkey can threaten to do the same in Iraq. Iran and North Korea can set their own terms for ending development of nuclear weapons, and on the other side of that coin, the nuclear powers that have signed the Non-proliferation Treaty can essentially ignore their commitments to build down existing arsenals. Such actions may not be cost-free in the larger picture, but they are "affordable" for the governments concerned.

Smaller and weaker nations in theory have the greatest interest in improving UN performance. They are the biggest beneficiaries not only of a collective security system, but also of collective efforts to pool resources for fighting disease, poverty and injustice. But they have touted UN ideals far more in word than in deed. Putting their own national and regional interests first, they have consistently blocked reforms that would strengthen Secretariat management and improve the efficiency of the General Assembly. They defend spendthrift projects and practice empty sloganeering for political gain. And they continue to abuse the principle of equitable geographic representation to put incompetents in UN staff positions and to make a mockery of bodies like the new Human Rights Council.

Somewhere between the big/rich and the small/weak nations, the emerging powers—BRICs and others—also stand to derive great benefit from the more stable world that the UN promotes. They are busy exploring the new possibilities that are opening to them as their wealth grows. China has expanded its activities in Africa, India has taken more of a leading role in the G-77 and G-20, and countries like Brazil and Mexico have joined in to prod for a greater say in international economic matters. These developments point in the right directions, but after the rhetoric is cleared away, much of the new drive seems to follow familiar patterns: Beijing's increased aid to poor countries is overly tied to Chinese suppliers; India has often been more interested in promoting its case for a Security Council seat than achieving broader goals; and Brazil, Mexico, Egypt and Pakistan have not paralleled their promotion of developing country economic ambitions with support for human rights in UN forums.

The popular will—up with the UN!

There is widespread popular endorsement of Roosevelt's "universal organization" that commits all governments to work together on global issues. According to a May 2007 report of the Chicago Council on Global Affairs from its poll of 14 countries representing 56% of the world's population, "Despite well-publicized disagreements over the role of the UN in world affairs, this survey shows that international opinion has coalesced around the notion that the UN should be the vehicle for conflict resolution and international cooperation on a wide variety of pressing problems."[16] The poll found that large majorities in many countries backed a more activist UN. This was particularly true in the US, where among other points, 72% supported a standing UN peacekeeping force, 75% backed UN authority to investigate human rights violations, and 83% favored UN use of military force to prevent genocide. Also, 60% of Americans surveyed thought Washington "should be more willing to make decisions within the UN even if it means that the US will sometimes have to go along with a policy that is not its first choice."

Solid majorities in America have consistently supported the UN since the mid-1970s, persisting through the 1990s into the millennium. Although the numbers dropped to just over 50% favorable in late 2006 according to data of the PEW Research Center, among young people under the age of 30, around 66% had a positive view of the UN.[17] With different questions, a Gallup survey of February 2007 found that almost 80% of Americans favored stronger UN participation in world affairs (close to half wanted the UN "to have a major policy-making role in world affairs while an additional 29% favor(ed) it taking a the lead policy role"), even though 65% of the respondents believed the UN is doing "a poor job."[18] In the same vein, analyzing a 2005 BBC poll, Steven Kull from the University of Maryland, concluded, "Apparently the United Nations is widely seen as a benign influence at the same time that more people have reservations about its performance."[19]

What is one to make of these numbers with reference to American foreign policy? One summation is that the public wants a UN that will use its authority to uphold UN Charter principles, by force if necessary in the case of more extreme violations. Few Americans, however, have a good grasp of why the UN hasn't taken the bit in its teeth to greater effect. News pundits over recent years have tended to blame "the UN," which they put across to their readers as a somewhat amorphous organization run by feckless Europeans, tin-pot anti-American dictators and/or a sinister Sino-Russian alliance. More serious national discussion of the issues has been drowned out more often than not by Washington politicians' UN bashing and the media's uncritical coverage of scandals.

Why does the UN get such a bum rap in the US? "The problem largely is a polit-ical time warp in the US Congress," wrote John Gerard Ruggie in 1996—his insight is as valid today as it was then.[20] Thanks in part, he noted, to the orga-nized anti-UN forces on the Washington stage and the absence of any counter-vailing pro-UN lobby, Congress in particular and the White House on most occasions have routinely ignored US public opinion in making policy.

Hype and hypocrisy

Ceremonial occasions at the UN present a different picture. World leaders including American officials are always mindful of public opinion, and invariably mouth high praise for the UN. Heads of State and Government gathered for the 60th Anniversary Summit at United Nations Headquarters in September 2005, for one typical example, declared: "We reaffirm our faith in the United Nations and our commitment to the purposes and principles of the Charter and interna-tional law, which are indispensable foundations of a more peaceful, prosperous and just world, and reiterate our determination to foster strict respect for them."

These warm endorsements of Charter principles are honored haphazardly at best. Many national representatives, like children who cross their fingers behind their backs, harbor unvoiced reservations when they sign on to such declarations. A few on the far margins, the governments of Myanmar and Zimbabwe for exam-ple, have no conceivable thought of bringing their practices anywhere near to UN norms. A large number of governments accept chunks of the Charter, but selec-tively ignore the parts of it that don't fit back home—they have no intention to alter political, cultural or religious behaviors that differ significantly from UN standards. Failure to call governments to account for violation of Charter norms is one of the most serious blind spots in UN practice. We shall delve more deeply into this problem in later chapters.

The core group of UN boosters—West Europeans, Canadians, New Zealanders and Japanese—are reasonably sincere in their commitment to work for a stronger UN. This is not surprising, since the Charter incorporates their values, and their populations strongly support multilateralist approaches to world affairs. The US ought to be counted in the same group, but it is not—President Bush was less than straight at the 2005 Summit when he spoke of helping to "fulfill the prom-ise of the United Nations," given that he had appointed an Ambassador who had publicly declared international law to be contrary to US interests and derided the UN in the most scornful terms.

Virtually all governments, in much the same robotic way they praise the Charter, express support for UN reform to close the gap between expectations and results. It is, after all, easier to speak in favor of improvements in UN performance than it is to change one's own behavior or policies. The collapse of the Berlin Wall inspired a torrent of ideas to take advantage of the end of superpower rivalry and reconstruct the UN to do what it was originally supposed to do. There has been an unending series of studies on, and proposals for, improving efficiency, strengthening management, and modernizing UN bodies, among other things, to make the Security Council more representative of today's world as opposed to the world of 1945 when it was designed.

But there has been little consensus on substance and priorities. Governments fight among themselves over what reform means, and many UN bureaucrats resist change in almost any form. As Harvard's Samantha Power wrote in early 2007, "UN member states and UN civil servants have grown practiced at pointing fingers at one another."[21] Although, as Power observed in her article, progress will require both sides to work together, the more fundamental fact is that underneath it all, changing the structure and procedures of the organization won't force changed behavior on the member states.

Reform—waiting for Washington

Public support for the UN has not produced corresponding government policies, except to some degree in western Europe and Japan. The UN's performance will not significantly improve until more member states take their own responsibilities more seriously, and invest more of their own political and economic capital to make the UN work better. But old habits die hard, and governments continue to find little incentive to change.

Change has to go beyond merely adopting multilateralism, which is in essence an approach, a tool of diplomacy. More important is the substance of the policies to be advanced through multilateral cooperation. The UN can play a strong role only if member states see it in their interest to work for the global system outlined in the UN Charter. That requires far-sighted vision, and in many cases willingness to forgo present advantage.

Over the near term, the outlook for real reform is grim. Recapping his experience as Kofi Annan's Chief of Staff, Sir Mark Malloch Brown in a June 2007 talk described how short-sighted and self-interested interactions between the US, Europeans and G-77 stifled progress on his watch. "The UN will continue to disappoint," he concluded, "until statesmen are willing to step forward and negotiate a new (UN) government which gives everybody significant confidence of ownership to stop acting like dissident shareholders using any means to stop the show, and rather be willing to allow an empowered accountable management to lead a modern UN under the strategic direction of (member state) governments."[22]

Echoing Annan's farewell speech at the Truman Library, Malloch Brown highlighted the crucial importance of the US. He did not mince words: "Reform in the UN (is) impossible without the United States." That is a central theme of this book. That is also why the US election in November 2008 will go far to shape the course of the UN over the years of the next American President's time in office. We will return to US policy considerations in the final chapter.

None of this is to say that nothing can be done until 2008, or that failure to put a multilateralist in the American White House in 2008 will doom the UN. The UN has become indispensable because, as Abba Eban observed, "With all its imperfections, the UN is still the main incarnation of the global spirit." It will continue to do an enormous amount of good work, and it will save millions more from the grip of poverty, disease and violence.

Our next three sections review the main parts of the UN—what works, what doesn't and why.

PART II

To Save Succeeding Generations from the Scourge of War

4

The Security Council and Its Achilles' Heel

o o o o o o o o o o o o o o o o o o o o o o o o o o o o o o o o o o o o
With all its defects, with all the failures that we can check up against it, the UN still represents man's best-organized hope to substitute the conference table for the battlefield.

—*Dwight D. Eisenhower, September 23, 1953*

The Security Council is a powerful instrument for peace—but only when substantial unity exists among its members. Absent consensus, the Council is little more than a meeting place.

The competition of national interests discussed in the preceding chapters can bring the Council to a standstill. The difficulty is compounded by the infamous veto power, enjoyed not only by each of the five Permanent Members, but often also by the NAM caucus through its ability in many cases to muster at least seven votes, enough to block a resolution.

In this chapter, we look at how the fractiousness of member states works to immobilize the Council, and explore to what extent these divisions can be overcome. There is no question that the US has the starring role, whether or not it commands Council support on any given agenda item.

The good news in the background

Since members do agree on many issues, the Security Council can and does undertake a tremendous program of work to keep the peace.[23] As of August

2007, Council-mandated peacekeeping missions are on the job in 16 countries, staffed by nearly 100,000 personnel with an annual budget of well over 5 billion dollars. A further 11 political and peacebuilding missions are also deployed in the field, two International Criminal Tribunals are in session with Council authorization, and Council committees monitor sanctions regimes imposed on several countries as well as a counter-terrorism coordination mechanism. In addition to those operational activities, the Council is working with major powers and the IAEA to address nuclear proliferation with respect to Iran and North Korea; is engaged with the new Peacebuilding Commission for post-conflict recovery; and has a number of other continuing items on its plate from trafficking in small arms and light weapons to the security implications of climate change.

The operations mandated by the Security Council save innumerable lives every day of the year, and the Council itself is the central actor for what in President Eisenhower's words (quoted above) is still "with all its defects ... the best organized hope to substitute the conference table for the battlefield." Council deliberations shape global cooperation on conflict prevention, management and resolution. Its positive contributions—which we will take up in more detail in the next chapter—should be kept in mind as we address here the criticisms leveled against it.

The deficiencies are real, and we have to ask why the Council hasn't been able to cope better with the challenges of Kosovo, Iraq in 2003, Darfur, Myanmar, and Iran's nuclear ambitions. Inability to resolve these and other critical security and human rights problems has cast a dark shadow over the UN itself. The Council is the UN keystone, but it is considered by many serious analysts to be "ineffective," even "broken." How does this unfortunate state of affairs come about?

The problem is not lack of legal authority. The UN Charter gives the Security Council virtually absolute powers—the Council is the global prosecuting attorney, judge, jury and police department rolled into one. The Council is empowered to act on behalf of all UN members, require the cooperation of all member states and use all necessary means including military force to compel compliance with its demands or to intercede in any situation of its choosing.

Authority to act, however, is not enough to guarantee action will be taken.

Vetoes—who casts them and why

The simplest way to stop the Security Council in its tracks is for one of the Perm-5 to exercise its veto, a device intended to assure no group would be able to marshal the Council's powers against the interest of one or more of its major members. In that sense it works—China for example would block any unwanted consideration of a Taiwan issue; the US would veto any proposed action against its Cuba embargo; Russia would not allow intervention in Chechnya; and so on. In practice, the mere threat of a veto usually keeps an item off the Council agenda, although sometimes members will force a Council debate to draw attention to an issue and embarrass the vetoing country. (The veto power does not extend to procedural matters, so it cannot be used to block an item from Council discussion.)

Over the 17 post-Cold War years from 1991 through mid-2007, only 19 resolutions have been vetoed. The US has cast the great majority with 13 vetoes, of which 12 killed measures critical of Israel. The anti-Israeli items had been pushed to a vote over US objections by the NAM caucus, acting essentially at the behest of Arab states, but emboldened as well by the world-wide sympathy for the plight of the Palestinians. Aside from defending Israel, the only other time the US voted 'no' was to keep US peacekeepers in Bosnia immune from the jurisdiction of the International Criminal Court—one of those instances where the majority compelled a vote, hoping the US would relent, but welcoming the spotlight on the issue when Washington held fast in splendid isolation.

Britain and France have not cast any vetoes since 1990. In 2002/3, however, the French (and Russian) threat to veto any resolution approving America's invasion plan for Iraq was a major factor in the acrimonious Council debate at the time.

China acting alone has vetoed two resolutions, both times intending to punish countries for maintaining diplomatic relations with Taiwan. In 1997, because of Guatemala's good relations with Taiwan, China blocked a resolution to send a peacekeeping mission to monitor implementation of the peace agreement that had ended civil strife in that country. This Chinese veto angered many governments, and Beijing responded to the pressure by working out a secret compromise with the Guatemalans that soon permitted passage of the resolution. The second Chinese veto in 1999 denied renewal of a preventive peacekeeping deployment in Macedonia, which also had relations with Taiwan. In this case, support for the peacekeeping mission itself was not especially strong, and the veto stood.

In an unusual move, China and Russia in January 2007 vetoed a resolution criticizing human rights violations by the Myanmar (Burmese) Government on grounds the situation could not properly be considered a threat to international peace and security, and therefore should not be on the Council's agenda. This, the only multiple veto cast since 1989, represented in part Sino-Russian concern that the US and the European members of the Council are too willing to intervene in the domestic affairs of others, not least because both Beijing and Moscow are sensitive to criticisms of their own human rights performance. When international demands for action against the Myanmar junta mounted in October 2007, the two did go along with a statement that the Security Council "strongly deplores the use of violence against peaceful demonstrations in Myanmar," but they continued to block a resolution, which would have been seen as a much stronger response than a mere statement.

By itself, Russia is something of a Council wild card and has used its veto power in a calculated way to bolster its claim to world standing. Moscow cast vetoes on Cyprus issues twice, first in 1993, to keep finances for the UN peacekeeping force on a voluntary basis, and again in 2004 to block a resolution encouraging a referendum vote on the island in favor of a UN peace plan. By most lights, neither of these issues went to the heart of any major Russian security concern: the first veto saved Russia a relatively small amount of money, and the second curried favor with Greeks.

The more consequential Russian exploitation of its Perm-5 veto has involved Serbia, and in particular the issue of Kosovo. It is true that Moscow has cultural ties with its fellow Slavs and has promoted a close relationship with Belgrade, but Serbia is distant from Russia's periphery, and the two are not part of any broader alliance. In 1999 Moscow prevented Council authorization for air strikes to deter Serbian repression of ethnic Albanians in Kosovo, so NATO proceeded "illegally" without Council approval and its bombing campaign eventually forced the withdrawal of Serbian armed forces from Kosovo. Russia then acquiesced to a UN occupation force for Kosovo, but in 2007 again threw a spanner in the works by threatening to veto a UN-sponsored plan for the independence of Kosovo. Moscow's stance in favor of existing territorial integrity has many precedents, but in this case its open thwarting of the UN/US/EU proposals intensified the difficulties of avoiding another cycle of violence.

Stealth vetoes—by disagreement or indifference

With or without veto threats, security problems fester in the absence of a Security Council consensus on what to do. The worst case was Rwanda, when well over half a million people were slaughtered while Council members dithered. Something of the same happened in the early days of the Darfur tragedy, before pressures started to mount for Council intervention. In Rwanda especially, the missing ingredient was leadership, in that Washington and other Council members had the evidence, but no Ambassador stood up in the Security Council to describe the genocide for what it was until hundreds of thousands had been killed. In Darfur, when the political temperature got high enough, as mentioned in a previous chapter, all the key players then accepted the need for more forceful action, but jockeyed for ineffectual resolutions that would do least harm to their particular interests in Khartoum.

The Council also drifts when loyalties to one side or another in a given conflict pull Council members in opposite directions. For example, too many countries have too much at stake in their relations with Pakistan and India to try to force progress on the open sore of Kashmir. On a lesser scale, the same is true in the case of Cyprus, divided since 1974. Despite thirty years of intensive UN-led negotiations to reunite the island, lobbying by the competing parties has staved off outside political pressures that might well have produced progress toward a solution. For another example—minor to all but the population of Western Sahara—it has long been an open secret in Council corridors that the future of that disputed territory will not be resolved except on terms acceptable to Morocco because few member states want to offend Rabat, even though the local independence movement, known as the Polisario Front, has ostensible support from a sizeable, if fluctuating, group of nations.

The most difficult and potentially dangerous situations for the Council arise when Perm-5 members are at odds over a threat involving possible military conflict that could spin out of control. In Kosovo, the risks of escalation were relatively low since Russia, the Perm-5 member with the strongest objections, was not immediately threatened by the NATO bombing, and Serbia was otherwise isolated. In the case of the US/UK invasion of Iraq in 2003, other Security Council members had no interest in military involvement themselves, but ethnic conflicts, insurgent forces within Iraq, and threats to regional stability all intensified the crisis. Having snubbed the Council in the beginning and then found itself unable to get on top of security within Iraq, Washington has had little success in trying to form a "coalition of the willing" for peacebuilding there.

The Security Council was also split by difference on how to stop North Korea and Iran from acquiring nuclear weapons. In the case of North Korea, the Council voted strong sanctions after Pyongyang exploded a nuclear device in October 2006, but the six-party (China, Japan, Russia, the two Koreas and the US) negotiations continued to stall. The Council and the governments leading the talks with the North Koreans did not get in synch until the US softened its position in 2007 and met bilaterally with the North Koreans—agreement then followed to disable the main North Korean reactor at Yongbyon, and American experts went to the site in November 2007.

As for Iran, negotiations to persuade Teheran to stop enrichment and open its nuclear facilities to IAEA inspections have been led by the Perm-5 plus One, that is the Perm-5 plus Germany. The US has taken a hard line throughout, arguing for tough Security Council sanctions to force unconditional Iranian agreement. The Bush Administration's "axis of evil" characterization of Iran's government has been paralleled with leaks suggesting that Washington is preparing a military strike to destroy Iranian nuclear facilities. The Europeans, while favoring diplomacy, have supported less rigorous sanctions, but Moscow and Beijing have objected to any such measures, demanding more time for diplomacy to work out the basic proposal for supplying uranium fuel to Iran in exchange for an end to the Iranian program. A CIA study in 2005 found Iran unlikely to achieve a nuclear weapon until about 2015.[24]

The inability of the Council to maintain a consensus has allowed Teheran to play off Moscow against Washington, while talking tough itself about equal rights to nuclear technology. Against the background of its miscalculations on Iraq, the Bush Administration has been criticized for believing it can strong-arm Iran into submission. By the same token, many also fear unilateral US military action would not only inflame the situation in the region, but probably also fail to take out Iranian facilities, redoubling Iranian determination in the process.

Scandals and oversight—where the buck should stop

Lack of leadership for the Council's oversight responsibilities in two particular episodes has also sullied Council-mandated operations, and by extension, grievously discredited the UN itself. Council members in essence abdicated their duty and let the UN Secretariat take the full rap for the oil-for-food program rip-offs that benefited Saddam Hussein and for the sex scandals that hit UN peacekeeping forces in the Democratic Republic of the Congo (DRC) and elsewhere.

In the case of the DRC, a Council discussion in mid-2003 could have saved hundreds, perhaps thousands, of innocents from exploitation. At that time, credible reports were appearing with evidence of sexual abuse by UN peacekeepers in the DRC, but Council members remained silent, and UN bureaucrats bumbled. A series of cover-ups and half-hearted investigations left little changed for months until a definitive UN report in January 2005 at last laid the problems bare—not only in the DRC, but in other countries as well; not only involving military personnel, but also civilians; and not only since 2003, but for a decade or more. The Security Council held its first-ever meeting on the subject May 31, 2005.

The stain on the Security Council record looks all the blacker in light of the mandate it approved for the DRC peacekeeping mission, which reads in part: "to assist in the promotion and protection of human rights, with particular attention to women, children and vulnerable persons." The reprehensible disconnect arose because in line with long-standing practice at the time, neither the Council nor the Secretariat nor the peacekeeping force commander was made clearly accountable to monitor personnel performance and enforce discipline. Political niceties had for years inhibited the Security Council from imposing unambiguous lines of responsibility. So, when the damning reports came in, the US along with other Council members turned blind eyes, happy to let the problems be swept under the rug—until the crescendo of complaints from media and civil society became too loud to ignore.

Laxity in the Council's oversight role also permitted the egregious errors of the sanctions regime against Iraq through the 1990s, including its oil-for food component. The US had written the original resolutions such that it could veto any change in the procedures, and for over a decade Washington used this lever to keep the focus on stopping any Iraqi import of military commodities with very little regard for the impact on Iraqi civilians or the flow of corrupt money to Saddam Hussein. These issues will be discussed in more detail later in this book.

"The buck stops here"—President Truman famously kept this sign on his desk to indicate he accepted ultimate responsibility for the deeds of his government. When it comes to peace operations, the buck stops with the Security Council. The Council did not act on the authority vested in it to set the terms for the oil-for-food sanctions and the DRC peacekeeping program. The Secretary General's passivity contributed to the problems, but that does not absolve Council members from their obligations.

Legitimacy, credibility and reform—talk is good

Proposals for Council reform surged to the fore in the 1990s and have become a prominent feature of UN summit agendas and annual General Assembly sessions. The debate proceeds on four major tracks. The first and most widely publicized topic is demand for change in Council membership, including both broader representation and revision of veto powers. On a second track, issues like Darfur and Kosovo have led to proposals for instituting a "responsibility to protect" populations at risk. Third, on the other side of the intervention coin, there is an effort to codify rules for the use of force, intended to deal with situations like that which arose in Kosovo and Iraq when major-scale military actions were unleashed without Council approval. Finally, the operational scandals and misfires have precipitated calls for stronger management of activities mandated by the Council. Only the last mentioned reform subject is likely to see significant change in the short term.

Expanding Security Council membership is the hottest of the reform issues, and governments who feel entitled to a permanent seat are lobbying hard. Two main arguments are advanced, both related to world changes since the Council was set up with 11 members in 1945 and expanded to 15 in 1965. The first contention is that of Japan and Germany, both of which assert that since they now pay a goodly share of Council costs, they should have a full voice in its decisions. They have a point in that after the US with a share of 26%, Japan pays 17% and Germany 9%, both ahead of four Perm-5 members: the UK at 8%, France at 7%, China at 3% and Russia at only 1% (these assessments, similar to those for UN general budget dues, are set by a formula based primarily on each country's GNP).

A more telling source of discontent is the Council's "legitimacy," namely the complaint advanced by many member states that the Council as now constituted is no longer representative of the world it purports to regulate. Emerging powers like Brazil, India, Pakistan, and South Africa along with several others believe they too should be given permanent seats to ensure regional input to Council decision-making. A wide range of countries, small and large, also find the veto power undemocratic as well as unrepresentative, and have proposed that it be circumscribed or eliminated. While there is an obvious validity to all these criticisms, the prospects for reform at this point are dim. Each of the candidates for a permanent seat has significant opposition, those who have the veto want to keep it, and any one of the Perm-5 can veto the Charter amendment that would be needed to change either the composition of the Council or the veto procedure.

Given the improbability of change in the Council's structure, a number of countries and NGOs have pressed for so-called "Cluster II measures," meaning steps which could be implemented without the need for a Charter amendment. In general, these involve measures designed to increase transparency of Council deliberations and to engage non-Council members in Council activities. The Council has moved in these directions with more regular briefings on Council discussions and a greater readiness to listen to the views of others before making final decisions. But many say the Council has not gone far enough, seeing the Perm-5 as jealous of their prerogatives and therefore leery of "too much" openness.

The second major theme for Council reform centers on action to rescue populations from criminally repressive governments. The proponents of a stronger interventionist approach in places like Darfur have scored important successes, even if they are still far from resolving the issue. The High Level Panel set up by Kofi Annan developed language which in effect puts the international community's "responsibility to protect" persecuted populations ahead of the principle of non-intervention in the internal affair of sovereign nations. (The protection concept is called R2P by insiders.) The R2P principle was endorsed by the 2005 UN Summit Declaration, although as the continuing agony of Darfur has demonstrated, talk is cheap and does not readily translate into action when governments are pulled off course by political and economic considerations.

On the third reform track, Annan's High Level Panel also propounded draft guidelines for the use of force across international borders. Although the Panel's set of principles were broadly acceptable, the US and a number of other major countries remain unwilling to sign away any of their flexibility to decide when and how to use military force. The Bush Administration in particular insists on its right to take whatever preemptive action it may deem necessary for self-defense. The issue has lost much of its intensity as the Security Council confrontations of 2003 recede from memory, but the need for some common understanding of such guidelines is central to a more comprehensive world security system. The debate, therefore, will not go away—nor should it.

Finally, many of the continuing calls for management reform touch on Security Council operations. The Brahimi Report, addressing the peacekeeping disasters of the 1990s, cogently outlined the need for clearer mandates, rules of engagement that explicitly protect civilians and adequate force to do the job. Adoption in 2000 of the Brahimi guidelines and their observance in Council practice—most of the time—has gone far to make Council operations more effective. And in response to the recent revelations of sexual abuse in peacekeeping operations, the Secretary General, backed by a General Assembly resolution, has instituted a zero tolerance policy which is now in effect and has resulted in forceful responses to allegations of misconduct. Auditing of Council-mandated operations remains weak however, and in general. it is far from clear that the Perm-5 yet accept responsibility for the kind of monitoring necessary to prevent the next big scandal.

Toward a more effective Security Council

Can the Security Council be made more effective? Absolutely! It is bound to work better if Washington, representing the Council's most powerful member, replaces America-first lordliness with team leadership.

Can the Council's structural defects be fixed? Not in the short term. But they can be mitigated if Washington adopts a more far-sighted approach and makes the necessary investment in diplomacy.

There are two prerequisites for successful American leadership of the Security Council. The first is a substantive foreign policy that makes sense to other democracies, above all the Europeans and Japan. It does not mean abandoning readiness to use force when necessary, but it does mean support for the rule of law in international affairs, priority attention to the protection of human rights, meaningful commitment to arms control and disarmament, joining the mainstream on environmental problems like global warming, and greater compassion for the poorer nations on our planet. The list of specifics is woven throughout this book and repeated often elsewhere: signing on to treaties like Rights of the Child, CEDAW, Law of the Sea, and the Comprehensive Test Ban; revitalizing the Nuclear Non-proliferation Treaty and a follow-on to the Kyoto Protocol; supporting the International Criminal Court; providing more development aid with fewer selfish conditions on its disbursement; and observing human rights norms of priority concern to the mainstream democracies.

The second prerequisite has already gained much attention, namely, the way Washington deals with other capitals. Multilateralism, diplomacy, state-craft—whatever the label, the heart of the concept is cooperation and mutual respect. Kofi Annan captured the practical aspect in a March 2005 speech to the UNGA: "If you need the help of others to achieve your objectives, you must be willing to help them achieve their objectives." Not the style of the Bush Administration!

A new American face on the Security Council will not of course banish the veto, an expedient that in any case, Washington itself relies on to protect the interests of Israel. The red lines of the Perm-5 will remain in place on issues that involve their domestic affairs or gut security concerns. The key to mitigating the undue influence of the veto threat is diplomatic leadership. In general, Perm-5 members do not want to be seen as frustrating the will of the international community by abusing their privilege, and skillful diplomacy can often exploit this factor to find a "work around." Beijing's negotiated retreat from its veto of the mission to Guatemala in 1997 was a case in point.

There has been much debate over the problem of Council legitimacy. A certain measure of resentment at Perm-5 prerogatives is real, but legal purists tend to overstate the political importance of both broader representation and the requirement for Council approval of cross-border military operations. Use of force that has clear humanitarian motivation will enjoy solid international support regardless of what countries are on the Council and whether or not a Perm-5 member vetoes—as demonstrated arguably by NATO's Kosovo operation. As for the Iraq debate in 2003, where international support was weak for the proposed US invasion, idealists might decry the Security Council's inability to stop a global superpower in its tracks, but that was simply not going to happen in the real world.

The more salient measure of progress toward world order was not that the US prevailed with its Iraq invasion, but rather that Washington felt obliged to try to get the Council's approval—and that a majority refused to go along with American bullying.

5

UN Tools for Peace—Political Missions, Sanctions, and Military Operations

o o o o o o o o o o o o o o o o o o o o o o o o o o o o o o o o o

The pursuit of peace and progress cannot end in a few years in either victory or defeat. The pursuit of peace and progress, with its trials and its errors, its successes and its setbacks, can never be relaxed and never abandoned.

—Dag Hammarskjold, UN Secretary General 1953–1961

Peacemaking is not as complicated as it sometimes sounds. The UN's basic strategy is plain common sense: prevent conflict if it can; seek peaceful solutions to disputes when possible; use non-lethal weapons before resorting to military force; and build or rebuild communities to remove the sources of conflict. Arms embargos and economic sanctions are tools that can be used to complement military peace operations or as tactics on their own.

UN peacekeepers have negotiated 172 peaceful settlements and helped 45 countries to move from conflict to free elections since 1945. In mid-2007, the UN had about 100,000 personnel in the field on peace missions. The numbers of armed conflicts and states "hosting" conflict has decreased markedly over the last two decades, but demand for peace operations remains high—the International Crisis Group in September 2007 was still monitoring about 60 situations of actual or potential armed strife.

This chapter examines the tools developed for UN peace operations. After 60 years experimenting and a record of mixed results, what now works, what doesn't and why?

Interventions—when and how to answer calls for help

The Charter gives the Security Council "primary responsibility for the maintenance of international peace and security." There is a long history of differing interpretations over what constitutes a threat sufficient to require or permit Security Council intervention in a sovereign nation. If armed conflict is not seen as likely in a given situation, other organs of the UN are generally expected to deal with disasters and problems meriting international attention or assistance—human rights violations, for example, in the first instance trigger debates and Special Rapporteur investigations under the purview of the Human Rights Council and the High Commissioner.

Since the Cold War's end, the Security Council has been not only more able but also more willing to consider interventions. In the 1990s, Council members began to accept that armed action could be necessary to assure delivery of aid to civilians caught in the middle of conflict, and the ill-fated peacekeeping mission to Somalia in 1992 was the first UN military operation authorized for the specific purpose of protecting humanitarian aid deliveries. Adoption of the 2005 Summit Declaration gave the Council a stronger mandate to intervene based on its "responsibility to protect" populations at risk, but this is still subject to narrow interpretations by the Perm-5. In 2000, the Council debated AIDS as a threat to international peace and security in Africa, and in 2007 it took up Climate Change as a global security threat, although neither exercise went beyond rhetorical encouragement. In 2007, China, Russia and G-77 representatives all expressed concern that debates of such topics lay outside the Council's proper jurisdiction.

When the Security Council does decide to take up an issue, it has a range of available responses from hot air to hot war. The lowest level of action, just putting an item on the agenda for a debate or hearing, can improve a situation by stimulating unwanted attention to a government that is threatening the peace or violating human rights. It has of course less impact on arrogant dictators, shadowy terrorists or isolated regimes like Myanmar and North Korea. The next Council escalation is issuance of a Presidential Statement—an official expression of concern agreed by a Council majority including the Perm-5. It usually gets the attention of the parties involved, but it has considerably less weight than a resolution.

Council adoption of a formal resolution signals serious intent. Even if the wording only calls upon the parties to seek peaceful solutions, the Council will normally follow up to consider whether additional action on its part might be required. The Council's options include requesting reports from the Secretary General, encouraging specific governments to play more constructive roles, and authorizing a civilian peace mission, as for example it did in January 2007 for Nepal to help implement a peace agreement between the government and insurgents.

Jawing—the political dimension

When an opening exists for mediation or negotiation, the UN is a uniquely qualified candidate for the job. It is above the fray, neutral, experienced and backed by the Security Council. In practice, these qualifications are sometimes diminished by perceptions that the US or another Council member has pulled strings behind the scenes, but at the end of the day, there is rarely an alternative more acceptable to the parties than a "good offices" mission in the name of the Secretary General.

In high visibility situations, the Secretary General himself will participate as Ban Ki-moon has done in Darfur. Or, a distinguished statesman may be dispatched, as was the case when Lakhdar Brahimi was called in to negotiate formation of a post-conflict government in Afghanistan in 2003. Usually, however, the Secretary General, drawing primarily from the ranks of professional diplomats, designates a Special Representative (SRSG), who serves outside the limelight, shuttling back and forth between the parties involved. In many cases, the Special Representative will establish an office in the field, as has been done recently in Somalia and Iraq, as well as Nepal. Less often, SRSGs are integrated with a field peacekeeping mission as was the case in mid-2007 in Afghanistan, Burundi and Sierra Leone.

The UN Secretariat's Department of Political Affairs (DPA) provides substantive and administrative back-up for peace envoys and political missions. Though small, DPA has a well qualified staff of analysts and experts to advise the Secretary General and his Representatives in the field. DPA is also the focal point for coordinating electoral assistance—a relatively new service, which has played important roles in transitions from conflict or when outside support is necessary to assure the integrity of an election. The DPA Electoral Assistance Division since its inception in 1992 has responded to over 100 requests from member states (as well as from non-members Palestine, Kosovo and Western Sahara) for help with elections.

At the tail end of the process, the political input of an SRSG office can make a significant contribution to post-conflict recovery. One small example of such a "mission accomplished" was the Special Representative in Bougainville, Papua-New Guinea, who monitored implementation of a peace agreement, supervised a weapons disposal program and assisted with elections and constitutional amendments before closing down the UN office there in 2005. For the more typical, larger and more complex settings, the UN continues to grapple with ways to mobilize and integrate the political, economic development, and social programs required to put a nation back on its feet.

Sanctions—palliatives or real medicine?

Imposition of sanctions escalates action from jawing up to the next level by imposing coercive measures to interrupt commerce, travel or financial flows. Carefully targeted sanctions of this sort were used with apparent success to require the Libyan Government to respond to demands that it produce suspects for trials and compensation for victims in connection with bombings of a French airliner and PanAm Flight 103 over Lockerbie, Scotland in 1988. However, the traditional notion of using sanctions to economically cripple a country or bring its leaders to their knees has generally been discarded because it rarely if ever works. Attempts to impose a trade blockade are too easily undercut by smuggling and in practice tend to punish ordinary citizens far more than officials in charge, who are the primary targets.

The more limited concept of "smart sanctions" has proven useful, if not always decisive, to apply political pressure, as in the case of Libya, or to constrain the fighting and funding capabilities of governments or non-state actors. The word "smart" describes measures designed to impact specific individuals or enterprises. They include seizure of assets, interception of funds transfers, prohibitions on travel of named individuals, and cutting off sales of high value natural resources, such as diamonds, timber and rare minerals, used to fund armed forces. An arms embargo is also an early option that can be tried to impede the flow of military material to protagonists in a combat zone, but it tends to be near meaningless whenever there is a remote or porous border at hand.

The issues surrounding sanctions in conflict areas are nicely illustrated by the history of the struggle between Angola's government and the rebel UNITA movement after a peace agreement fell apart. In 1993, the Security Council found UNITA responsible for the failure of the accord. The Council went on to impose a series of sanctions (the first against a non-state actor) that by 1998 covered UNITA's trade in weapons, petroleum and diamonds. Lax enforcement, however, and the complicity of neighboring governments left UNITA virtually untouched by the embargos—its diamond sales may have exceeded $3 billion through the 1990s to finance its military force.

Then in January 1999, Canadian Ambassador Robert Fowler took over as Chair of the Security Council's Sanctions Committee for Angola and set about putting teeth into the process. He traveled to the area and demanded cooperation from governments and the private sector, including the top officers of De Beers and others in the world diamond industry. Using information from a panel of experts established by the Council, Fowler began to "name and shame" government and business figures implicated in violations. This startling departure from diplomatic nicety had a catalytic effect and doors began to close for UNITA. While a definitive assessment is not possible, the Canadian diplomat's aggressive enforcement of sanctions appears to have seriously impaired the rebel military machine, opening the way for a second peace settlement and the conversion of UNITA to a political party. Fowler showed what had to be done to make that kind of sanctions regime effective.

When Liberia's corrupt leader, Charles Taylor, was found to be helping the ruthless RUF movement (known for cutting off hands of opponents) in neighboring Sierra Leone, the Security Council took Fowler's model to heart and for the first time imposed sanctions on a government for violating an embargo earlier imposed on another country. After Taylor was finally driven out of Liberia and later brought before a special tribunal for supporting the RUF's war crimes in Sierra Leone, the Council maintained sanctions to disrupt arms flows, financing and travel that could have contributed to a rebel resurgence.

In severe problem states with remote borders—such as Somalia, Sudan, and the Democratic Republic of the Congo—smuggling continues to defeat arms embargos. A frank UN Expert Group report in early 2005 on the DRC described networks of arms flows and criticized both Rwanda and Uganda for maintaining "security arrangements with leaders of armed groups in the embargoed regions." Policing borders is difficult in the best of circumstances, and in the real world, most arms embargoes will have only limited effect on fighting capabilities.

Regrettably also, the effectiveness of programs to deter illegal exploitation of natural resources is still questionable. Organizers of the "Kimberly certification process" to prevent sales of "conflict diamonds" claim broad success, but monitoring by Amnesty International and another NGO, Global Witness, has continued to show that only a few companies selling diamonds in the US and Europe can provide a "meaningful account of their policy to prevent the trade in diamonds from regions of conflict."

What does it add up to? First, the imposition of sanctions can send an important political message, a shot across the bow from the Security Council. And second, sanctions will have a significant effect if, and only if, the Council follows through with a sustained effort to obtain compliance by all parties involved. In sum, sanctions, no matter how 'smart,' are unlikely by themselves to stop violence, and make sense only as part of a determined political or military campaign.

Oil-for-food—the sanctions success that backfired

The Oil for Food (OFF) sanctions program in Iraq was probably the last of its kind, but a brief recounting is useful here for what it says about sanctions as a tool, about relations between the UN Secretariat and the Security Council, and most importantly about the hypocrisy that has characterized Washington's handling of UN issues for the last twenty years. The Security Council devised the Oil for Food (OFF) program in 1995 to alleviate the suffering of Iraqi civilians from blanket UN controls then in place over Iraqi trade. OFF permitted carefully regulated oil sales with proceeds to be used for civilian needs, but the Saddam regime corrupted the program to fill its own pockets while still able to paint the sanctions as cruel punishment of the Iraqi people. World opinion continued to judge the UN measures as inhumane, even after it became obvious Saddam was diverting funds to build opulent palaces instead of hospitals,.

The Security Council itself was deeply split. France and Russia (with one eye on future commerce, according to US diplomats), along with China and most non-permanent members called for easing of sanctions on humanitarian grounds. Washington, in part driven by conservative hard-liners in control of Congress, pursued strict implementation. Just how hardened US leaders had become was exemplified by then-Ambassador to the UN Madeleine Albright, who when asked in May of 1996 about keeping sanctions in light of reports that half a million Iraqi children had died, responded, "This is a very hard choice, but the price we think, the price is worth it."[25] Within a day or two, she disavowed the statement, but the sanctions stayed, and US government experts examined every Iraqi import contract to assure no military equipment was purchased with the money.

Did the Iraq sanctions work? Post-invasion investigations showed the US/UK scrutiny of Iraqi imports had indeed accomplished the program's primary disarmament objectives. Saddam had been unable to pursue development of nuclear or other WMDs, and the sanctions effectively hobbled the Iraqi military. Ironically, Iraq's unwillingness to cooperate with UNSCOM allowed hawks in Washington to capitalize on far less reliable sources for the wildly inaccurate intelligence information used to justify the war in 2003.

But both the Security Council sanctions committee and the US officials involved had knowingly allowed oil smuggling outside the UN program as well as Iraqi sales contract manipulation, including padded prices and kickbacks. These illegal activities put billions into Saddam's pockets, but went unchallenged by the US because Washington chose to focus only on blocking the flow of military equipment to Iraq. Washington in fact explicitly exempted Turkey and Jordan from any punishment for their lead roles in violating the UN sanctions to facilitate oil smuggling that earned over $5 billion for Saddam. Businessmen in the US, Australia and elsewhere made fortunes buying oil or selling goods while playing the kickback game to get big contracts—only a few have since been indicted and convicted.

When the story broke, Washington helped steer all the blame to the UN, keeping mum on its own role. A conservative US Senator charged that "the UN" had steered "billions" to Saddam, and the media hammered away for months on alleged UN culpability, along with demands for investigation. Eventually, a multi-million dollar UN inquiry led by US banker Paul Volcker did show that the UN Secretariat had not exercised effective control and that the UN official in charge appeared to have taken a de facto bribe of about $160,000. What got lost in all the coverage was the extraordinary complicity of the US government, which knew about the money flows to Saddam and deliberately turned a blind eye, abdicating its responsibility as the lead actor on the Security Council sanctions committee. The episode did irreparable harm to the UN's reputation and that of

Secretary general Annan while Washington escaped with a clean bill in the public eye—the result no doubt delighted the Bush Administration on both counts.

Peacekeeping in military uniform—taking off the gloves

The term "peacekeeping" is used widely today as an umbrella term for peace operations that have military or police functions at their core. Peacekeeping missions proliferated like spring flowers in the early post-Cold War days, with scant attention given to the doctrinal confusion and problems of command and control that contributed to the catastrophes of Somalia, Bosnia and Rwanda. In 2000, a chastened Security Council adopted recommendations from the highly regarded Brahimi Report. Today's peacekeeping missions are more robust, more flexible and more ready to use force than in the past to defend civilians or control rogue militias and gangs.

The consent of parties involved is still the preferred prerequisite for deployment, and armed peacekeepers in the field normally use force only as a last resort in self-defense or to protect civilians. The instructions or "mandate" contained in the Security Council resolutions that authorize a blue helmeted force specify its mission. The units may be assigned to assist in implementing a peace agreement, to prevent conflict or the spill-over of conflict across borders, to stabilize conflict situations, and/or to "lead states" through post-conflict transition to a stable democratic government. Armed UN peacekeeping missions, authorized to use necessary force, have also been deployed to protect the delivery of humanitarian aid to civilian populations and refugees.

To manage and support UN missions ordered by the Security Council, the UN's Department of Peacekeeping Operations (DPKO) has evolved into a substantial and professional enterprise. At its core, a Military Division is responsible for planning, assembling forces, and directing current operations, as well as for training and evaluation. The Division also oversees a Standby Arrangements System, which maintains up-to-date information from over 90 potential troop-contributing countries with details of available troops, equipment and response times. A Civilian Police Division manages the police personnel that have been a central feature of almost every peacekeeping operation since 1988. Other capabilities include a 24/7 Situation Center, an Office of Mission Support with a sizeable depot of contingency supplies at Brindisi, Italy, a Mine Action Service to coordinate programs for elimination of land mines, and a Best Practices Unit to assure attention to the cross-cutting issues of gender, human trafficking, HIV/AIDS, criminal law/judiciary, and "DDR," a recent acronym for disarming, demobilizing and reintegrating former combatants.

As of mid-2007 DPKO had more military personnel deployed to the field than any other entity except the US Government—over 73,000 military, supplemented with 9,500 police and over 20,000 civilians, including local hires. In 2006, it airlifted over 800,000 passengers and 160,000 metric tons of cargo, and operated over 200 hospitals and clinics. In a word, UN peacekeeping is a big operation. And a relatively cost-effective one at that—a US Government Accountability Office study on peacekeeping in Haiti estimated that UN operations there cost less than one half the price of a comparable US military deployment.

Participation of non-UN forces under their own colors has expanded peacekeeping capabilities and proved a useful approach in many cases. Such 'hybrid' missions have included fully integrated operations under one command (as was the case in Kosovo and Haiti); two separate, but coordinated military commands (for example the UN and French units in Cote d'Ivoire); sequential operations with UN units following or preceding a cooperating force (as happened in Timor-Leste); short-term military intervention, as when a UK force essentially rescued West African peacekeepers held hostage in Sierra Leone; and a civilian-military division of labor in Afghanistan where EU and US forces carry the military burden and the UN has a civilian political office.

The option of hybrid operations offers both military and political advantages. It helps governments face opposition at home to placing their troops under foreign command; alleviates (or masks) concerns over the adequacy of UN commands or the quality of UN commanders in the field; and can assure the participation of seconded force commanders in military decision-making. It also spares military units the trouble of changing, or even just repainting, equipment to be compatible with UN-organized units.

The Security Council can also authorize a country or regional organization to undertake a peace operation on its own steam. This pattern has precedents, as when the US and its allies were authorized to take all necessary means to free Kuwait from Iraqi occupation in 1991. In recent years, the strain of demands for finance and personnel has led the Council to encourage stronger participation by regional organizations, including NATO, the Organization of American States (OAS) and the African Union. In 2004, for example, the Council authorized a Multinational Interim Force in coordination with OAS and the Caribbean Community to stabilize Haiti, pending later take-over by a Blue Helmet force.

Efforts to give the African Union (AU) a greater role in Darfur and Somalia have been problematical at best; at worst, they have given the Security Council an excuse not to take more meaningful action. The small, if valiant, AU force (AMIS or African Mission in Sudan) sent to Darfur by terms of a 2004 peace agreement (without Security Council participation) was woefully inadequate to provide any real security for civilians in Darfur. In 2006, the Council approved a UN force to work in tandem with AU units in Darfur, but deployment was conditioned on Sudanese government acceptance and delayed pending the green light from Khartoum until at least 2008. In 2007, the Council approved an African Union force to protect the transition government which moved into Mogadishu, Somalia after Ethiopian military elements drove out Islamic militias. Regrettably in this case as in Darfur, the African Union lacked resources to field adequate forces, wealthy Security Council members offered little help, and the situation on the ground was practically unchanged.

Once a genuine peace agreement is attained, continuation of peacekeeping force presence is typically critical to facilitate post-conflict recovery. Over the longer term, sustaining the peace requires a much broader approach: institutions of government must be rebuilt, a democratic political process has to be energized, and economic activity has to be kick-started. While UN agencies, such as UNDP, UNHCR and WHO, have generally been willing to participate, systematic long-range planning and coordination has been a hit or miss proposition in many cases.

Recognizing the magnitude of post-conflict tasks, the 2005 UN Summit declaration proposed a Peacebuilding Commission (PBC), which was established the same year by resolutions of both the Security Council and the General Assembly. The Commission, up and running since early 2006 with representatives from 31 countries, is an "advisory body" tasked to "bring together the UN's broad capacities and experience" to assist countries emerging from conflict. The PBC has access to a separately administered Peacebuilding Fund, which had pledges of over $200,000,000 as of August 2007. Sierra Leone and Burundi were chosen as the first two countries for PBC assistance, with $35 million initially allocated for programs in each to help catalyze reconstruction. Subsequently, the PBC approved grants to support peace talks in Cote d'Ivoire and the Central African Republic, and in October 2007, Secretary General Ban declared Liberia eligible for PBC reconstruction funds, simultaneously directing the UN Mission there to begin consultations with the government and potential local civil society partners.

Reality checks—what works, and what are the limits?

Peacekeeping works when the objective is clear and the force is matched to the task. That sounds straightforward enough, but in the Security Council setting, the twin requirements can easily get lost as members states seek to make political hay or avoid unwanted commitments. Defining success or failure depends on what goals the Council hopes to achieve when it approves a peacekeeping mission. Then too, circumstances change and early success measured by lives saved may give way to backsliding or stagnation with a return to violence—Haiti, Timor-Leste, and Cote d'Ivoire are three of many examples.

On the good news side, there is reason to expect the peacekeeping disasters of the 1990s will not be repeated. The Council and Secretariat have learned the basic lessons, at least to the extent that they now recognize the folly of underestimating threats and therefore work hard to establish the facts on the ground. Generally, peacekeeping missions are far better equipped to deal with potential adversaries, as for example in Haiti where they have taken action to suppress armed gangs, and in the DRC where they have clashed with marauding militias.

That does not mean, however, that the Council is prepared to intervene with decisive force in every case. In Darfur and Somalia, as noted above, the African Union forces deployed in 2007 were far too small to even protect deliveries of humanitarian assistance. In the DRC, a much more powerful UN force was deployed, but its scope of action was limited and reports emerged of killings and rapes taking place within a few hundred meters of UN peacekeeper detachments. To be fair, it should be said that the Council is inevitably constrained by political and financial realities which leave it at times with no better option than token intervention to show international community concern and signal possible future escalation.

The most recent of the missions deployed in the classical format to supervise a truce between hostile nations is UNMEE, on the job in Ethiopia and Eritrea since September 2000. It is a good demonstration of the continuing utility of UN peacekeepers since tensions have remained high, and the presence of Blue Helmets has helped deter the resumption of fighting. Relations between the two countries were further strained by the Ethiopian military intervention (with apparent US support) in Somalia in 2006/7, so there seems little chance of early positive change.

Five such "classic" peacekeeping missions have virtually permanent status: three related to Arab-Israeli conflict, one on the Pakistan-India border and one in Cyprus. All have been in the field since before 1978, and the two oldest will soon mark 50-year anniversaries. The "failure" to achieve lasting peace lies not at the feet of the peacekeeping forces, but rather with the leaders of the nations directly involved along with those of the international community. The UN soldiers on the ground represent "success" in that without their presence as a buffer and fact-finding truth squad, chances of violent confrontations between the contending parties would be considerably greater.

In recent years, the majority of peacekeeping missions have been deployed to deal with internal strife or civil war rather than cross-border conflict between nations. Peacekeepers have unquestionably played vital roles to restore or maintain order in Kosovo, Haiti, Sierra Leone, Burundi, Cote d'Ivoire and Timor Leste. However, with the exception of Kosovo thus far, initial peace agreements foundered and bouts of serious unrest followed. According to the research of Oxford University's Paul Collier, the chance of reversion to conflict in these kinds of situations is roughly 40%—not surprisingly, the risk is higher if security arrangements are not complemented by political reform and some measure of positive economic growth.[26]

The establishment of lasting stability and functional governments remains a difficult proposition. It can be done—examples of past success include Namibia and Central America, where internal conflicts influenced by the Cold War wound down in the late 1980s. Peacekeepers monitored truce agreement implementation, facilitated elections and gave confidence to reconstruction efforts. Other major examples of reasonably successful transitions include Cambodia, and Angola on the second try after the first peace agreement between the government and UNITA failed to hold up.

Experience and more realistic expectations have refined the scope and nature of peace operations. The man in charge of DPKO, UN Undersecretary General Jean-Marie Guehenno, in an April 2004 International Herald Tribune op-ed essay, specified four overarching principles:

- "no UN engagement in hot wars ... If there is real campaigning to be done, then military coalitions, such as the one the Security Council authorized in the Gulf in 1991, should be used."

- "partners count ... arrangements (with regional organizations) have their complications, but the neighbors and friends have an interest in seeing problems through. In a world of short attention spans, there is a need for those who won't turn away."

- "no job without the tools ... the men and women in uniform from developed and developing countries alike; the specialized military support services from those countries that have them, the financial resources, the strategic force reserves, the sustained commitment. Without that support, the peace will invariably fail."

- "stick with it until peace takes root ... Peacekeeping operations must be linked to a longer term plan for achieving ... stability."

At heart, Guehenno's article is an appeal to developed countries—the US, Europe, and Japan—for greater participation and support. They are the heavyweights with the financial resources and military muscle to make peacekeeping work, when they have the political will. That is a matter of leadership and vision, not an issue of the Council's structure and legitimacy, or of the competence of the Secretariat.

Guehenno's plea is especially pertinent to the countries seemingly trapped in cycles of recurrent civil strife. Most of them are in Africa, where the African Union has put itself forward in principle as chief provider of peacekeeping forces, although it cannot possibly train, pay and deploy them on its own tab. Elsewhere, nations like Haiti and Timor Leste also need more help to get on a stable footing. They are among the poorest countries on the planet and cannot possibly improve their lot without external assistance. Washington can afford to do much more for them—and should.

The greater challenge to the panoply of US interests is the Middle East. In Afghanistan it is now evident that Washington shot itself in the foot by snubbing the Security Council, invading the country with its closest allies to depose the

Taliban, and then not following through on promises to assure reconstruction of the country. Although Washington subsequently engaged NATO and attracted considerable development aid, the outlook is still bleak. The Bush Administration burned too many bridges to be able to assemble the kind of team needed to have good chances anytime soon for rescuing Afghanistan from the resurgence of drug lords and Taliban mullahs so painfully evident in 2007.

The difficulties presented in Afghanistan are huge, but they pale in comparison to the peacebuilding problems of even more enormous complexity facing the world in Iraq and the Arab-Israeli confrontation. While UN peacekeepers and humanitarian agencies have made major contributions in the Middle East since 1945, the UN is not in any position to take the lead. These challenges will have to be addressed by US-led coalitions of the powerful working with representatives of the peoples directly involved. The UN, however, remains uniquely well-placed to play a valuable complementary role by providing the blue flag's neutral political 'cover' whenever appropriate for negotiations or operations on the ground.

6

Seeking Justice—International Law, Courts and Tribunals

Public international law, which purports to regulate the relations between nations, is an amorphous, slippery thing. The traditional cynical view is that if you are a big, strong nation, international law does not exist unless and until you choose to believe that it does.

—Charles Foster, English Barrister, 2003[27]

What does it mean that the US invasion of Iraq was "illegal?" Why aren't the perpetrators of genocide in Darfur or the tyrannical rulers of Myanmar and Zimbabwe being hauled before a court? And, given America's proud traditions, why isn't the US government trying to strengthen the rule of law internationally?

International law is a mystery to most ordinary people and fraught with problems for the experts. This seems especially true of the legal framework for global peace and security, where vital gaps remain, interpretations of basic elements are contested and enforcement is uncertain at best. All in all, the situation is a far cry from familiar models of national systems with legislatures, prosecutors, police, courts and prisons working in concert.

This chapter looks—in layperson terms—at major elements of international law, and why it has been so difficult to evolve accepted rules for the use of force between nations, including guidelines for intervention to deal with governments that grossly violate human rights. We also take up the role of international law in fighting international terrorism.

The UN Charter—giant leap forward

The UN Charter fashioned a radically new legal foundation for international security. Its provisions for the first time definitively reversed the centuries-old acceptance of the right of military conquest by requiring all members to refrain from "the threat or use of force against the territorial integrity or political independence of any state."[28] The Charter also advanced international law for equal rights and self-determination, underpinning the wave of decolonization that soon redrew global boundaries. And its creative language paved the way for the path-breaking endeavors that followed to secure universal human rights and freedoms, and to combat discrimination based on race, sex, language or religion.

The Charter did a remarkable job of pulling the pieces of international law together for a fresh start after World War II. The International Court of Justice Statute annexed to the Charter codified the sources to be used by any court adjudicating inter-state disputes:

- international conventions and treaties;
- international custom as evidenced by current practice among states; and
- general principles of law recognized by the world's major legal systems.

Treaties are an indispensable feature of relations between states, regulating the world's trade and communications, governing the conduct of diplomacy, setting international standards for the environment, and so on. They are generally self-contained in the sense that the signatories to any particular treaty agree to be bound by its terms, and where appropriate, they set up implementation review panels or specify penalties for non-observance. Disarmament agreements and regional defense pacts like NATO or ANZUS are in treaty form and comprise major components of the international security system, as do compacts such as the Antarctic Treaty, the Outer Space Treaty and those establishing nuclear free zones on planet Earth.

The muscle of international law for resolving serious disputes between nations is the UN Charter. Use of force is allowed under the Charter only for self-defense, spelled out in Article 51, or by decision of the Security Council. There is a limited safeguard for individual states in Article 2.7, which forbids UN intervention in matters "essentially within the domestic jurisdiction of any state." Over the last three decades, this injunction has lost much of its weight where human rights abuses are involved, and a vigorous debate continues on what circumstances should trigger outside intervention.

The Charter also carried forward the pre-war international court, revising its statute and renaming it the International Court of Justice (ICJ), to adjudicate international cases. The Security Council is directed to see that "legal disputes should as a general rule be referred by the parties to the International Court of Justice." As good as this approach may sound, however, the ICJ has to a large degree operated in an ivory tower, with little influence on the real world of armed contention.

Use of force—legalities and politics

The Charter language on international security was grounded in hopes of ending the kind of military aggression that had bedeviled the globe in the run-up to World War II—epitomized by Hitler's invasions of Poland and France. Since 1945, the Security Council has responded with military force to only two cases of similar aggression—North Korea's advance into South Korea and Iraq's seizure of Kuwait. In other instances when victim states might reasonably have sought UN assistance, the lack of unity among Security Council members precluded a military response under UN aegis. Examples include the Suez crisis of 1956 and Soviet invasions of Hungary and Czechoslovakia. Some would also point to the Turkish military occupation of part of Cyprus as well as to the US military invasions of Grenada and Panama, although the Turks were treaty guarantors and claimed the need to defend ethnic brethren, and the US in both cases reestablished democratic government and withdrew in short order.

During the Cold War, proxy conflicts also lay outside the Charter's reach. In struggles from Greece to Vietnam to Angola and all manner of places in between, East and West fought for influence or outright control, not by invading with tanks across borders, but by proffering support, often covertly, to proxies and like-minded comrades. The Security Council was hamstrung by the veto, and the few General Assembly resolutions of disapproval had virtually no effect. Where the Soviet Union and the US did not perceive important interests at stake, a measure of cooperation was possible, most notably perhaps in 1960 when the Congo descended into chaos, and the peacekeeping force (ONUC) was formed at Secretary General Hammarskjold's request to the Council. Similar "truces" between the US and the Soviet Union permitted the Security Council to impose sanctions on Southern Rhodesia in 1966 and on South Africa in 1977. Broad political opposition to apartheid made the actions feasible at the time, and they were not treated as precedents to override national sovereignty for humanitarian objectives.

The cases of Bangladesh in 1971 and Cambodia in 1978 illustrate the difficulties of sorting through morality, legality and Cold War politics. When secession-minded groups in Bangladesh (then East Pakistan) won electoral victories, Pakistani military units from the geographically separate western wing of the country moved in to take control and began reprisal killings. Although over 9 million refugees fled into India as the slaughter continued, the Nixon/Kissinger Administration in Washington, blinded by its Cold War alliance with Pakistan, tried to dissuade Delhi from acting. Indira Ghandi's government hesitated, but when Pakistan attacked air bases on Indian territory, Delhi launched military operations, which quickly liberated Bangladesh from the genocidal pogrom. India withdrew after installing a government with officials previously elected.

As for Cambodia, following a series of armed clashes on its border, Vietnam invaded in late 1978 and toppled the genocidal Pol Pot. The US, suffering from a Vietnam War hangover, ignored reports of Khmer Rouge atrocities and denounced Hanoi's action. China, which had been currying favor with Pol Pot, unleashed a punitive military expedition into northern Vietnam. The Soviet Union supported Vietnam and blocked Security Council action, although it was unable to prevent passage of a General Assembly Resolution that retained the UN seat for the murderous Khmer Rouge. Unlike India in Bangladesh, Vietnam stayed on for a decade, maintaining hegemony there as well as in Laos.

The Indian and Vietnamese invasions had no Security Council approval, and might therefore be deemed illegal, although the governments asserted self-defense. When all is said and done, there seems no question that both actions had as much humanitarian justification as the Kosovo case. Neither intervention, however, was given such credit by an insular West, caught up in the political imperatives of the Cold War.

Self-defense—or is it?

The legal exercise of self-defense under Article 51 has proved more complicated than it would appear on the surface, at least to laypersons. The language allows a state to act alone or in concert with allies if the Security Council fails to do its duty. In both Korea and Iraq/Kuwait the US was unquestionably prepared to invoke Article 51 and take military action if the Council had declined its request for approval. When in 1967 Israel launched preemptive attacks to forestall an imminent invasion of its territories by Arab armies then on the move toward its borders, neither the Security Council nor the General Assembly was willing to condemn Israel for aggression despite the strong anti-Israeli sentiment of the day.

Many situations are far less obvious, and there is a self-evident need to prevent Article 51 from being called into play without adequate justification. When Israel in 1981 bombed an Iraqi nuclear weapons facility under construction, the Security Council unanimously censured the strike, rejecting arguments that the threat was sufficiently material or imminent to require armed action. In the 1962 Cuban missile crisis (involving a potentially threatening deployment of Soviet missiles, but where armed attack did not appear imminent), the US declined to explicitly invoke Article 51 and relied on national discretion.

In the wake of Al Qaeda's attacks on the World Trade Towers in New York, the Security Council demonstrated broad support for America's use of force in response. But the Bush Administration, perhaps fearing delays, chose to rely on Article 51 and proceeded outside the UN framework with its military action against Afghanistan and Al Qaeda. The Security Council in effect then ratified the US course.

The Security Council did not, however, see Iraq in the same light. The US decision to depose Saddam Hussein by force provoked a crisis of credibility for the UN and international law. President Bush made clear he would order military action regardless and declared that Council failure to approve a US-led invasion of Iraq would render the UN "irrelevant." When the Council demurred, the US marshaled its "coalition of the willing," deposed Saddam forthwith and occupied Iraq.

Most commentary around the world deplored the US decision to act without approval from the Security Council. Many experts deemed the US-led invasion to be a violation of international law, and Secretary General Annan said as much when pressed in a 2004 BBC interview, observing that the action was "not in conformity with the UN Charter," and thus, from the UN point of view, "it was illegal." He had strong backing from many who argued the US should abide by the UN Charter, and that what to do about Saddam's transgressions was properly a matter for the Council as a whole to decide, not just one or two of its members.

Washington gained public support at home with claims that Saddam was developing WMDs and had connections to Al Qaeda. This tack suggested the US was acting in self-defense, in line with the new US doctrine of preemption, although mounting a massive military invasion to counter uncertain Iraqi threats could not be said to meet traditional requirements for a showing of necessity and proportionality. (These criteria were brilliantly articulated and enshrined in international law by America's Daniel Webster in 1837 after a British raid sank a US ship used for supplying rebels in Canada.) As events unfolded, the US arguments were exposed as grossly exaggerated, if not trumped up, when post-invasion investigations found no factual basis for them. The US was left with only one justification, elaborated largely after the fact: the humanitarian one of freeing Iraq from tyranny and installing a democratic government.

Was the American invasion illegal or not? From most perspectives, it was in fact in violation of the UN charter and therefore illegal, but there is no definitive ruling on the application of international law. And there is no practical question of enforcement, since the only police power is the Security Council, where of course Washington has a veto.

Humanitarian intervention—devil's details

The problem of dealing with Saddam Hussein's murderous regime in Iraq reflected the lack of agreed guidelines for humanitarian interventions. As noted above, the principle of non-interference in domestic affairs held sway at the end of World War II, even though the UN Charter had broken new ground by promoting "respect for human rights and for fundamental freedoms for all." But the Charter envisioned achievement of these goals through cooperative endeavor between nations rather than through enforcement by the Security Council.

In 1948, the Universal Declaration of Human Rights and the Convention on the Prevention and Punishment of the Crime of Genocide initiated obligations of member states to be proactive on issues of human rights. The Genocide Convention requires signatory states to prevent the crime and to see that those responsible—rulers, officials or other individuals—are punished. It does not explicitly authorize any particular action against a state, but it has within it the concept of confronting a government for illegal actions against its own citizens.

The US waited until 1988 to ratify the Genocide Convention, and then did so with reservations and interpretations that in effect exempt the US itself from application of the key article which provides for ICJ action. As a result, the US can never be charged (unless it agrees in advance) before the Court, but neither can it bring charges against any other country unless that country agrees in advance—for example, Washington cannot press a case against Sudan for its actions in Darfur without Khartoum's OK. In sum, America's ratification of the Convention is essentially symbolic.

The more general Universal Declaration of Human Rights set many new standards, but not legal requirements to implement them. Later conventions on political and economic rights, racial discrimination, apartheid and discrimination against women further defined norms for government behavior. The 1975 Helsinki Accords, although binding only on the signatory countries in North America and Europe, took matters another step ahead by imposing obligations not only to respect human rights and fundamental freedoms, but also to permit outside monitoring of performance. These developments have strengthened universal pledges to observe human rights, but regrettably, the UN institution primarily responsible for enforcement, the UN Human Rights Council (formerly the Human Rights Commission) has been made dysfunctional by UN member states which stack its roster with unqualified representatives.

In early 1991, the aftermath of the Gulf War raised a major question about the legality of using force for humanitarian intervention. After his defeat, Saddam Hussein sought to reestablish authority over the northern part of Iraq and wreak vengeance on its Kurdish population. The Security Council passed Resolution 688 demanding that Iraq "immediately end this repression." The US, UK and France took military action, imposing a "no-fly zone" over the north of Iraq, which together with covert military support to the Kurds effectively kept Saddam out of the area. Paris soon withdrew its participation, but the US and UK continued to protect the Kurds and later added a southern no-fly zone over areas where Saddam had brutally repressed Shiite uprisings. There is no consensus on whether, in the absence of more explicit Council approval, the US/UK/French action was legal, or illegal but legitimate, or neither.

The first clear case of "legal" humanitarian intervention conforming to UN Charter principles for use of force was that of Somalia in 1992/3. The Security Council authorized military action to assure delivery of aid to starving civilians caught in the crossfire of internecine warfare. US marines splashed ashore unopposed and made it possible for UN assistance operations to go forward. There was, however, no political settlement, and US forces withdrew after failing in the disastrous "Blackhawk down" effort to arrest a rebellious warlord. Somalia descended into failed-state chaos from which it has yet to recover. Later UN interventions in Bosnia and Rwanda were also legal, having Security Council approval, but failed even more disastrously in their execution.

The issue of humanitarian intervention again confronted the Security Council in 1998/9, when Belgrade under Slobodan Milosevic used armed force against ethnic Albanians in the Serbian Province of Kosovo. Despite a broad consensus that the Serbian army was carrying out unjustifiable acts of ethnic cleansing, Russia sympathized with its Slavic brethren and blocked any Security Council use of force. NATO then commenced a bombing campaign, which eventually compelled Belgrade to withdraw its military and police from Kosovo. Moscow later acquiesced to establishment of a UN protectorate, UNMIK, to administer Kosovo. The Independent International Commission on Kosovo, established at the initiative of the Prime Minster of Sweden, concluded that the military operation in this case, while illegal, was nonetheless morally justified and hence "legitimate."

Through 2007, the gap between legality and legitimacy had still not been closed. In Darfur there was no question that thousands of innocent people were dying from attacks of militia supported by the Sudanese Government. But China, Russia, and a number of Arab states as noted earlier prevented Security Council intervention, and the US waffled for weeks before using the word genocide. Matters were delayed so a panel appointed by the Secretary General could examine whether genocide was in fact the case.

As the issue played out, the UN panel ruled there was evidence of "crimes against humanity," but not a pattern of genocide. The vapidity of this pronouncement underscored that international law meant little or nothing in this case and the fate of Darfur would be decided by how capitals weighed their own national interests. The terrible consequences for the people of Darfur and the stumbling international effort to assist them are discussed in more detail in Chapter 8.

Accountability—who's to judge?

The trials at Nuremberg and Tokyo firmly established the principle that individuals should be held accountable for acts as dreadful as those committed by the fascist regimes before and during WW II. After the trials concluded, however, no standing court was set up to hear cases against individuals, and in practice prosecution for crimes against humanity was left to national authorities, such as the post-dictatorship trials in Greece and Argentina.

Many despots were never prosecuted. One who floated for years above the law was Chilean dictator Augusto Pinochet, despite the fact that thousands were murdered and tortured under his rule in the 1970s and 80s. Starting with his arrest in London in 1998, however, authorities in the UK, Spain, France and Chile pressed to try him for crimes against non-Chilean nationals and to seize his assets held abroad. Failing health kept Pinochet from trial in Chile until his death in 2006, but the success of the legal efforts against him advanced the principle of universal jurisdiction—that grave human rights crimes can be prosecuted any-where in the world. The most aggressive example of efforts to break new ground was a 1993 Belgian law, which granted national courts authority to try "serious violations of international humanitarian law," but it was repealed in 2003 under pressure from governments, especially Washington, which feared application to American leaders for involvement in controversial actions such as supporting Pinochet in Chile or invading Iraq.

Incontrovertible evidence of atrocities shocked the Security Council into estab-lishing separate ad hoc tribunals for the former Yugoslavia (ICTY) and for Rwanda (ICTR) respectively. The Council's action signaled new resolve to put teeth into long dormant provisions of international law. The two courts, still in progress as of mid-2007, have brought several criminals to justice. Both, how-ever, have been criticized for excessive delays and costs.

In 2000, the Security Council approved a special court for Sierra Leone, which was duly created in 2002 with a mix of national and international participation. It effected arrests of numerous prominent individuals, brought its first case to trial in 2005, and indicted Liberia's exiled former President, Charles Taylor, for abetting crimes in Sierra Leone. Special arrangements were made after Taylor's arrest to hold his trial in The Hague so it would not be disrupted by former rebels or sympathizers.

The International Criminal Court (ICC), the first standing world court to prose-cute and try individuals for gross human rights violations, became a reality in 2002 over US opposition. By mid-2007, 105 countries had ratified the treaty, and the Court had active cases underway against alleged criminals in the Demo-cratic Republic of the Congo, northern Uganda, the Central African Republic, and Sudan. The US initially blocked Security Council referral of Dafur to the

ICC, but relented under public pressure and abstained (i.e., did not veto), allowing passage of the Council resolution to engage the ICC, which has moved against individuals in Khartoum.

President Clinton approved the ICC treaty, but it had no chance of ratification by the conservative American Senate. Under President Bush, Washington has adamantly opposed the Court, and aggressively sought agreements with other nations to exempt US military personnel. Since the US is not a party to the treaty, the ICC has no jurisdiction in America, but it could take up cases against Americans for crimes committed elsewhere. Washington has required a number of countries, as a condition for continuation of US assistance, to pledge not to allow ICC cases against Americans. It also initially refused to let American military personnel serve in UN-related activities unless exempted, until the revelations of misconduct by American soldiers at Abu Ghraib prison in Iraq led to at least temporary suspension of the policy in 2004.

The statute of the ICC, negotiated before September 11, 2001, does not specifically cite international terrorists for prosecution under its aegis. Its mandate, however, covers genocide, war crimes, and crimes against humanity—the last mentioned could include major terrorist conspiracies and acts such as the crimes committed by Al Qaeda under Osama bin Laden. Some have suggested the ICC is well suited for an anti-terrorist role, but US opposition to the Court in general and differences over such issues as the death penalty (excluded in ICC cases) bode ill for any early moves to give the ICC a more direct role.

International law and terrorism—casting the net widely

Terrorism became a serious international concern with the hijacking of planes to and from Cuba in the late 1950s. These and other incidents led to the Tokyo Convention on aircraft safety of September 1963. More skyjackings, including in 1968 the first by Palestinians, precipitated two further treaties, the Hague Convention against unlawful seizure of aircraft in 1970, and the Montreal Convention a year later aimed chiefly at sabotage, such as bombings aboard flights.

UN member states were shocked into more global action by the 1972 Munich Olympics incident in which Arab terrorists killed 11 Israeli athletes. But developed countries and the Third World had very differing perspectives, in particular on Palestinian issues, and for two decades, there was no meeting of the minds on a definition to distinguish between terrorists and freedom fighters. Nonetheless, the General Assembly slowly began to focus on acts of terrorism that a majority could condemn regardless of the motivation behind them. The persistence of international terrorism from a variety of organizations—the Red Brigades and Action Directe in Europe, the Japanese Red Army, and Sendero Luminoso in Peru, as well as Al Qaeda in the Middle East—led to further agreements intended to protect diplomats, guard nuclear materials, improve security of travel, stop financing of terrorism and mark plastic explosives so they could be more easily detected.

Debate continues on a comprehensive definition of terrorism to avoid interpretations that allow terrorists to disguise themselves as well-intentioned patriots. General Assembly Resolution 49/60 in 1994 marked a sharp departure from the past, with straightforward language condemning terrorist acts and calling upon all states to cooperate to stop them. It contained a clear message that the ends no longer justified the means: "Criminal acts intended or calculated to provoke a state of terror in the general public, a group of persons or particular persons for political purposes are in any circumstance unjustifiable, whatever the considerations of a political, philosophical, ideological, racial, ethnic, religious or any other nature that may be invoked to justify them." This version has broad support, although it remains bedeviled by differing interpretations, and US conservative fears that it could be used against Israel.

The UN Charter makes no reference to non-state actors, but Article 51 on the inherent right of self-defense has provided a basis for legal use of force in response to terrorist armed attacks. Israel has cited the provision repeatedly, and the US invoked it in 1986 to justify strikes against Libya in retaliation for the bombing of the La Belle Discotheque in Berlin, which was frequented by US military personnel. Similarly in 1993 the US bombed Iraq for Saddam Hussein's alleged attempt to assassinate the first President Bush, and struck targets in Sudan and Afghanistan in 1998 after US Embassies were bombed in Tanzania and Kenya.

September 11, 2001—globalization of anti-terrorist law

The horrific events of September 11, 2001 put terrorism at the top of the Security Council agenda. The Council on the next day passed Resolution 1368, which upholds the right of self-defense and condemns the September 11 attacks "like any act of international terrorism, as a threat to international peace and security." It goes on to call for action against the perpetrators and their supporters, and to redouble efforts to suppress terrorist acts in general.

Some read Resolution 1368 as giving states new and wider latitude to use force against terrorists and supporters under the aegis of Article 51. Russia's President Putin interpreted it in this manner a year later when in a letter to the Council and OSCE alleging Georgian assistance to Chechen rebels, he asserted Russia may use its right of self-defense "as stipulated in resolution 1368."[29] What exactly is legal and what's not in such situations, however, remains uncertain.

Subsequent Council resolutions have imposed additional obligations on all states, including those who were not parties to the earlier anti-terrorism treaties. Resolution 1373 draws heavily from two conventions—one on suppression of terrorist bombings, the other on financing of terrorism—signed in the late 1990s, to make many of their provisions legally binding on all states. Resolution 1540 addresses measures to prevent the proliferation of WMDs to non-state actors. It passed unanimously, despite expressed concerns by some governments that treaty negotiations, as opposed to Security Council resolutions, would be the better way to create such law.

In sum, Security Council resolutions have intensified anti-terrorism priorities and made applicable parts of treaty law universal. Nonetheless, the global law enforcement effort to counter terrorists remains focused much as it was before September 11 on harmonizing legislation and coordinating national authorities. Not much will happen beyond this, as long as the US continues to rely on military actions of its own choosing, while declining to seek a broader role for the international legal system, such as the engagement of the ICC, which West Europeans, among others, would surely support.

The International Court of Justice—not just a paper tiger

The Charter defines the ICJ as the "principal judicial organ" of the UN. With its seat at the Peace Palace in The Hague, the Court has 15 judges, chosen by the General Assembly and Security Council to reflect geographic and cultural diversity, with no more than one from any country. The Court, which does not take up complaints against individuals, has two primary duties: to settle legal disputes between states submitted to the Court by the parties involved, and to give advisory opinions on legal questions referred to it by international entities, such as the UN General Assembly and major UN agencies. The ICJ has also been specified in hundreds of treaties to be the authority for resolution of disputes arising under the treaties themselves.

Over the years, the ICJ has exerted considerable influence on world affairs, despite the relatively modest number of major cases adjudicated at The Hague. It resolved disputes in several instances where tensions and tempers ran high, including fisheries in the North Atlantic, continental shelf issues in the Atlantic and Mediterranean, the frontier line between Burkina Faso and Mali, and the ancient Preah Viharn temple on the border of Cambodia and Thailand. Perhaps more important than such specific rulings, however, the Court's methodology and views have infused the concepts and practice of international law in general. For example, its treatment of a case brought in 1974 by Australia and New Zealand against French nuclear testing helped to frame problems of trans-boundary pollution, even though the case itself was declared moot when the French pre-emptively announced they would not set off explosions. Its 1975 ruling involving Western Sahara ended the doctrine of *terra nullius*, a legal principle which up to that time had been used to justify taking of lands from indigenous populations by conquest without just compensation. Indigenous Australians were able to successfully defend land rights in the Australian High Court in the 1990s.

There is in practice little need for enforcement of ICJ decisions, given that they are either advisory or taken up only with the prior acquiescence of the parties. The UN Charter in Article 94 (2) does, however, provide for referral to the Security Council to resolve problems arising if a state submits to the Court's jurisdiction, but refuses to accept its judgments. In any serious case, the Security Council can always invoke its broad powers under the UN Charter to take action if it so chooses.

The ICJ's second main function is to render advisory opinions at the request of UN bodies. Its most controversial pronouncement in this role came in 1996 when following a request for advice from the General Assembly, the Court ruled by an 8-7 vote that the threat or use of nuclear weapons would "generally be contrary to the rules of international law applicable in armed conflict, and in particular the principles and rules of humanitarian law." The Court added, however, that the threat or use of such weapons might be lawful in the extreme circumstance of self-defense with the survival of a state at risk. The Court finding has been ignored by states possessing nuclear weapons.

In 2004, again responding to a General Assembly request, the Court found Israel's barrier wall between Jewish and Palestinian settlements to be "contrary to international law." It also ruled that Israel was obliged to cease construction forthwith and to make reparation for damages, and that all states are "under an obligation not to recognize the illegal situation." The votes on these rulings were 14 to one, with the US judge dissenting. Construction of the wall continued unaffected.

The impact of ICJ advisory opinions, particularly these two highly contentious examples, is difficult to measure. On the one hand, some argue that since the major governments concerned pay little or no attention to such rulings, the Court is exposed as a paper tiger, and respect for international law is consequently diminished. Others point to the value of better-informed debate and the prospect that over time the weight of the judgments will be manifest as international law evolves. One indicator of progress will come, critics say, when judges no longer make rulings to accord with the policies of their own governments.

The ICJ remains a marginal player in the area of international peace and security. China and the US do not accept compulsory jurisdiction of the Court. While any government can submit a specific case, states that decline compulsory jurisdiction generally pursue other avenues. Referral to the Court of a politically charged, potentially violent, inter-state dispute is rare. The boundary quarrel between Ethiopia and Eritrea is the saddest recent example of a situation where, by all reason, tragic armed combat should have been avoided through judicial intercession.

Conclusions—The US vs. The Rest

Proponents of the rule of law can take heart from the advances made since 1945 and in particular over the last three decades. Human rights are firmly on the world's agenda and with the creation of the ICC, international law is being brought to bear as never before. But governments are still at the basic level of laying foundation stones. Difficulties include conflicts between principles such as responsibility for humanitarian intervention vs. non-interference in domestic affairs, unresolved issues such as the legal rights of indigenous peoples, widespread practices that don't conform to legal standards set forth in documents such as human rights conventions, and a decided lack of enforcement.

Conservative American distrust for international law remains a major bar to its strengthening. Once manifested in isolationism, the dogma has been propelled since the 1980s by theories of nationalistic "sovereigntism" and American exceptionalism, which in essence are fancy words for "America knows best." This nationalistic ideology has led the US to withdraw from compulsory jurisdiction of the ICJ, renounce the ICC, reject important global treaties, and put debilitating reservations on agreements it has ratified. In 2005 the US also withdrew from a Geneva Convention Protocol, which it had in fact originally fostered, to guarantee access of persons arrested in a foreign country to a consular officer from their home country. Foreigners facing possible death penalties in the US were invoking the protocol, resulting in delays or reconsideration of their cases, so the US government simply opted out—the rationale of American conservatives was that the US has the best legal system in the world and should not brook any distraction from abroad. In this case, it also forfeited the reciprocal right of Americans arrested abroad to make contact with their Embassy if arrested.

Moreover, aggressive Washington actions taken in the name of counter-terrorism since 2001 have been severely criticized. Human rights activists have sought to roll back the most egregious of the Bush Administration measures: redefining torture to permit cruel and degrading treatment of prisoners, maltreating prisoners at the US facility in Guantanamo, and "extraordinary renditions," the practice of clandestinely sending detainees to other countries where they could be interrogated or tortured in secret. Commenting on the Bush Administration argument that Geneva Convention norms for treatment of certain prisoners need not be followed in all cases, Peter J. Spiro found it to be "almost transparently driven by the sovereigntist premise that international law is more fiction than reality."

Notwithstanding conservative influence in Washington, surveys have consistently shown that the US public favors the international rule of law and endorses US participation in the ICC, even if it risks prosecution of Americans.[30] Influential American scholars and NGOs may yet be able to energize this favorable disposition to tip the balance back in the direction of UN Charter ideals. Until there is decisive change in the Senate as well as the White House, however, the American government will remain an obstacle to extending the writ of international law, leaving other western democracies and civil society to be the engines of progress on this score.

7

Arms Control—Disarmament in an Age of Uncertainty

○ ○

World military expenditure in 2006 was $1,204 billion ($1.2 trillion) ... The USA spent $528.7 billion ... In the period 1997–2006 world military expenditure rose by 37%.

—Press release for the Stockholm International Peace Research Institute (SIPRI) Yearbook 2007 on Armaments, Disarmament and International Security[31]

Spending on armaments of all types spirals upward, while work on halting the proliferation of WMDs—nuclear, chemical and biological weapons—has made only limited progress in recent years. One of the worst nightmares imaginable is terrorist detonation of a nuclear bomb in, say, New York, Cairo, or Sydney. And yet, in May 2007 representatives of 188 nations ostensibly seeking to strengthen controls against nuclear proliferation were still arguing over how to interpret the Nuclear Nonproliferation Treaty signed in 1968. Something is wrong with this picture.

There are a few brighter spots. A negotiating breakthrough in 2007 halted North Korea's nuclear weapons production, and thanks mainly to the push from civil society, efforts continue to restrict landmines and stem the flow of small arms to conflict areas. But the overall outlook is grim, given the threat from possible terrorist WMDs, the uncertainties of Iran's nuclear development program, and the full bore armaments programs of many governments.

This chapter describes the framework for global disarmament and sorts out the major themes that are dominating efforts to regulate arms and keep WMDs out of the hands of terrorists. We look at the impact of Washington actions which have put key arms control negotiations on hold because of the Bush Administration's distrust of multilateral cooperation and its differences with America's traditional allies.

Toward a global arms control system—work in progress

Guns or butter? The drafters of the UN Charter proceeded from the proposition that resources are better applied to social and economic development than to military purposes. They accepted, however, the reality that nations were not prepared to disarm completely, and so the Charter calls not for elimination of armaments, but rather for their "regulation."

Awed by the enormous destructive power of the atomic weapons dropped on Hiroshima and Nagasaki, the General Assembly used its first resolution on June 24, 1946 to establish the UN Atomic Energy Commission, tasked to promote the control of atomic energy for peaceful purposes and the "elimination ... of atomic weapons and all other weapons adaptable for mass destruction." It got stuck in the starting blocks when the US and USSR tabled competing proposals, and it simply ceased to meet after 1949 when the Soviets exploded their first atomic bomb. In 1952 the UN combined the Atomic Energy Commission with a co-existing forum for conventional weapons to form one Disarmament Commission (DC), which still meets regularly, albeit as little more than a tedious and ineffective talk-shop.

In his 1953 "Atoms for Peace" speech to the General Assembly, US President Dwight Eisenhower resuscitated the goal of limiting the use of atomic energy to peaceful purposes under international control. The initiative led to the creation in 1957 of what is today the International Atomic Energy Agency (IAEA) with its 'three pillars' of responsibility: nuclear verification and security; safety; and technology transfer. The IAEA, however, could not slow the development of US and Soviet nuclear forces, which produced the Cold War standoff known as MAD (Mutually Assured Destruction), based on the ability of both sides to destroy the other if either one launched a nuclear attack.

Nuclear have-nots demanded a voice in negotiations, and in 1958, the General Assembly enlarged the DC to all members of the UN. The NAM group induced the Assembly to designate the 1970s as a Disarmament Decade, hold the landmark first Special Session on Disarmament (SSOD-I) in 1978, follow up with a second Disarmament Decade for the 1980s, and organize two further Special Sessions. These high profile activities publicized the issues, but one well-respected analyst trenchantly observed, "What little of the UN disarmament debate has not been pure charade has been rankly hypocritical."[32] UN negotiations had few possibilities in any case, since Washington and Moscow held all the high cards in those days.

Trying to salvage some wheat from the chaff, the more sensible UN members managed at SSOD-I to set up the Conference on Disarmament (CD) with 18 participating governments as an alternative to the unwieldy and pompous Disarmament Commission. The CD from its inception evinced pride in independence from UN control.[33] It sets its own agenda and rules of procedure, although it gets its budget from the UN, its meetings are serviced by the UN, and the UN Secretary General appoints the Secretary General of the CD. Seeing where the action was, others pressed to join, and the CD membership grew to 65 countries by 2007, with more knocking at the door.

The critical foundations for preventing the spread of WMDs were laid when the US and Soviet Union agreed to support multilateral negotiations. Their collaboration led first to the Partial Test Ban Treaty of 1963 and then the milestone Nuclear Nonproliferation Treaty (NPT) of 1968. Shortly thereafter, in 1972, the CD produced the Biological Weapons Convention, and finally in 1993, the more stringent Chemical Weapons Convention was signed in a separate forum, to be administered by the independent Organization for the Prohibition of Chemical Weapons. In contrast to these positive trends, India conducted a controlled nuclear explosion in 1974, while Israel and South Africa covertly developed weapons of their own. (South Africa later gave up its program and destroyed its weapons, but Pakistan exploded a nuclear weapon in 1998 and North Korea did so in 2006.)

On a parallel track, the idea of 'nonarmament treaties' bore initial fruit with adoption of the 1959 Antarctic Treaty, negotiated by nations active in the Antarctic during the 1958–59 International Geophysical Year for scientific research. The treaty prohibited military activities, nuclear explosions and nuclear waste disposal. It was followed by the Latin American nuclear-weapons-free zone set up by the Treaty of Tlatelolco in 1967 (Cuba did not sign until 2002); the Outer Space Treaty of 1967; and the Seabed Treaty of 1972. The latter two combined the principles of non-militarization with specific injunctions against nuclear weapons, and both accommodated particular superpower defense interests in intelligence gathering and surveillance.

MAD no longer—the US/EU and Russia build down

Progress on global nuclear disarmament still awaits resolution of the dormant, but not extinguished stand-off between the US and Russia. The end of East-West confrontation made possible a significant reduction in the risk of nuclear war when the two powers stood down their MAD regimes by reducing the number of nuclear weapons and ceasing to maintain missiles on hair-trigger alert aimed at each other's cities. Skeptics, however, assert it would only take minutes for either side to re-target and fire missiles since both retain extensive capabilities. New Zealand has recently proposed a convention requiring that all nuclear weapons be taken off high-alert and a resolution to this effect passed November 1, 2007 in the UNGA disarmament committee with 124 supporters—the US, Britain and France voted no, while Russia and China didn't show up.

Presidents Bush and Gorbachev in the fall of 1991 agreed to cut back on certain tactical nuclear weapons and delivery systems. Unlike previous pacts, their bargain was based on a political commitment and not expressed in a detailed written treaty with provisions for verification. The initial bilateral undertakings developed into a broad set of programs for "cooperative threat reduction" to help the cash-strapped Russians and other states of the former Soviet Union build down and safeguard their nuclear facilities, including funds for redesign of nuclear power reactors and alternative employment schemes for Russian scientists, lest they hire themselves out to rogue states. In 2002 the Treaty of Moscow (also called SORT for Strategic Offensive Reductions Treaty) reduced the number of strategic nuclear warheads back to a level of between 1,700 and 2,200 for each side, although without an explicit verification mechanism or requirement to destroy weapons put into storage.

Expanding the nuclear threat reduction effort started by the elder Bush and Gorbachev, G8 leaders at their June 2002 summit meeting in Canada signed on to the Global Partnership against the Spread of Nuclear Weapons and Materials of

Mass Destruction. The Partnership has commitments for over $17 billion to work on destruction of chemical weapons stocks and dismantling of old Russian nuclear subs, as well as safeguarding of nuclear materials. The Partnership's performance, however, has been criticized for delays, and its timetable stretches years into the future for full implementation.

In 2006/77, however, a dark shadow was thrown over this promising picture of US-EU-Russian cooperation, when the Bush Administration announced its intent to deploy an anti-missile system in Poland and the Czech Republic. Washington called its plan important to protect against Iranian missile development, but Moscow sees it as intended more to contain Russia. Reacting strongly, the Russians have talked of scuttling the treaty limiting intermediate-range nuclear missile deployments, which would be a serious set-back to global disarmament goals. American critics allege the Bush plan involves questionable technology and is unnecessary, given the low Iranian capability at this time. But Washington has continued to press ahead, accepting the diminution of NATO-Russian arms control measures and nudging Russia into closer cooperation with Iran, as evident during an October 2007 visit by Putin to Teheran.

Outside Europe, the 1990s brought a measure of progress on nuclear non-proliferation. South Africa gave up its nuclear weapons program to sign the NPT in 1991, and the NPT itself was extended indefinitely in 1995. Nuclear Weapons Free Zones were agreed for Africa (Pelindaba 1996) and Southeast Asia (Bangkok 1997), adding to the path-breaking Latin American treaty and one agreed for the South Pacific in 1986. These treaties discouraged countries in the zones concerned from developing nuclear weapons, but lacking meaningful endorsements by the nuclear weapons states, the effect on transit through the zones or deterrence of potential attacks from outside their boundaries was more rhetorical than real.

Proliferation blues—Pakistan, India, Israel, North Korea, and maybe Iran and Al Qaeda

Progress on halting the spread of nuclear weapons slowed by the mid-1990s. Although, the CD forged agreement on the Comprehensive Test Ban Treaty (CTBT) to prohibit testing of nuclear weapons, it never got off the ground. Neither India nor Pakistan signed the treaty, and conservatives in the US Senate refused ratification on grounds that it unacceptably restricted America's defense options and was unenforceable. The Bush Administration does not support the treaty and China has yet to ratify it, although in point of fact, none of the Perm-5 has conducted nuclear tests for some years.

In 1998 Pakistan joined India as a self-proclaimed nuclear power, and both nations successfully tested atomic weapons that year. As of 2007, the two countries maintain their nuclear face-off, fueling concerns of an accidental launch and fears that religious extremists might somehow get their hands on a weapon.

On the brighter side, the North Korean problem appears "solved," although only after Pyongyang joined the ranks of nuclear haves by successfully exploding a device in October 2006. The Six Nation Process—talks between the two Koreas, the US, China, Japan and Russia—produced a deal in February 2007 to end the weapons program, and in July, the IAEA confirmed that the key North Korean nuclear facility had been shut down. The agreement followed a reversal of the Bush Administration's refusal to talk bilaterally with the North Koreans, and the positive results have been contrasted by many with the previous failure of the neocon "axis of evil" approach that precluded bilateral negotiations unless hard-line preconditions were met. Some might draw the lesson that once a state explodes a nuclear bomb, even neocons will come to the table.

The immediate nuclear danger, particularly in official American eyes, is the threat posed by possible acquisition of nuclear weapons by Iran or a terrorist group such as Al Qaeda. In 2003 IAEA exposure of Iranian programs to develop a uranium enrichment capability precipitated a flurry of efforts to tie Iran into a credible safeguards program that would prevent diversion for weapons production. Iran insists it is working only on peaceful uses of atomic energy, and has resisted EU and US demands to bring its program under stricter IAEA safeguards. EU countries offered trade and other benefits to Iran, but in 2006, Teheran announced success in uranium enrichment, and in December of that year the Security Council imposed sanctions against trade with Iran of nuclear materials and technology.

The standoff continued into 2007. In September at the UNGA, Iranian President Ahmadinejad adamantly defended Iran's "right" to nuclear technology and vowed the program would continue. Washington, for its part, will talk with Teheran only if the Iranian program is first verifiably suspended, while the Europeans generally support both talking and sanctions. The threat of additional Security Council measures is a major factor in the negotiations, although perversely in other UN forums, Iran has been able to retain considerable rhetorical support from NAM countries.

And what about terrorists? IAEA can't inspect Al Qaeda, and Osama bin Laden doesn't give a fig about the NPT. One of the scariest threats is the possibility Al Qaeda or another organization could obtain a nuclear weapon.[34] It cannot be ruled out that terrorists could get the capability to build a crude bomb, small enough to be transportable and powerful enough to kill hundreds of thousands if detonated in a major city. Advanced technology might again become available from the kind of covert network set up by the lead scientist for the Pakistani program, Dr. Abdul Qadeer Khan, before western government pressure terminated his operation.

The idea of 'suitcase bombs' is especially unnerving, although some experts have concluded that a terrorist organization could not construct a usable working nuclear bomb without assistance from a supporting state, in particular for obtaining the necessary fissile material.[35] Acquisition of such material is the terrorist's biggest problem, and on this score the world is vulnerable, since over 30 nations have stocks, some of which are not as well protected as they should be. Terrorists could conceivably also mount attacks to blow up existing power plants to release radiation, or explode a so-called 'dirty bomb,' that is, a conventional explosive with radioactive material wrapped around it to be dispersed by the blast.

Verification of the use and disposition of fissile material is the heart of IAEA's responsibilities, but it must be able to conduct meaningful inspections in order to implement the NPT protections. The CD has taken up a Fissile Material Cutoff Treaty (FMCT or 'fissban' treaty) intended to further curtail production of supplies adaptable for weapons use. The Bush Administration in a reversal of the earlier US position for a time stalled talks by objecting to verification provisions, but in 2006 called for a fresh start and tabled a version without verification measures. As of late 2007, an FMCT appears as distant as ever, hostage to not only disagreements over verification, but also to linkages with negotiation of other treaties, such as one on outer space coveted by Russia and China.

Why doesn't the Nuclear Nonproliferation Treaty work better?

The guts of the NPT was a deal whereby the five nuclear weapons states (NWS) agreed to pursue complete disarmament and to refrain from transferring war-related technology to non-nuclear weapons states (NNWS). For their part, the signatory NNWS foreswore acquisition of weapons, but retained an "inalienable right" to pursue peaceful nuclear energy programs. The IAEA is the watchdog charged to assure compliance with the NPT through a system of controls and inspections conducted under 'safeguards' agreements with NNWS. Inspections are voluntary so the IAEA can't bust down doors, although it can use intelligence information supplied by the US and others.

The NPT has worked up to a point. When it entered into force in 1970, there were five NWS (namely the US, UK, France, China and Russia), and now there are nine (the first five and three non-signatories India, Pakistan and Israel, along with North Korea, which may or may not have a bomb or two in storage), plus one suspected aspirant in the case of Iran. That is too many, but fewer than might have been expected. The good news is that 181 non-nuclear weapons states are still abiding by the treaty. To that extent, the treaty combined with complementary nuclear-free zone obligations has made possession of nuclear weapons unacceptable in many neighborhoods.

On the ground, there is in place a complementary set of arrangements intended to deter and intercept illegal transfers of nuclear weapons technology or materials, including missiles that could carry nuclear warheads. These systems apply to all illegal transactions, whether by state or non-state actors. Specific control regimes include the Zanger Committee of 35 nuclear exporting countries to apply IAEA safeguards to recipients; the Missile Technology Control Regime (MTCR); the Wassenaar Arrangement on Export controls, and the new Proliferation Security Initiative, put in motion by the US in May 2003 with about 80 participants as of 2007 cooperating to interdict shipments of WMDs, delivery systems, and related materials.

However, the NPT is flawed as a legal framework and despite the additional control arrangements, it cannot be adequately enforced. Its most fundamental loophole is that it gives every state the right to develop nuclear capabilities for peaceful purposes. And a peaceful program can at its end stage be readily converted into a weapons program, needing only high grade enriched uranium or plutonium—neither is easy to obtain, but not impossible either. Demonstrating the limitations of the enforcement framework, the Iraqis before 1991 submitted their peaceful program to inspections, and still successfully concealed facilities doing work on weapons. The big question in 2007 is whether Iran is doing, or trying to do, the same.

Politics and NWS defense policies have also weakened the NPT's foundations. For one thing, the international community has done little or nothing about the fact that India, Pakistan and Israel simply ignored the treaty to acquire their nuclear weapons, and political realities preclude any serious action against them in the near future. Western governments tend to view India and Israel as stable democracies unlikely to use their capability except in self-defense. The West also gives Pakistan's current (2007) autocratic military regime the benefit of the doubt, but many would question that nation's future stability. Israel occasionally makes veiled threats of reliance on its nuclear weapons, a tactic to warn its enemies and keep the West on its toes in the Middle East.[36]

The credibility of the big five nuclear powers on arms control is further compromised by their abiding refusal to take serious concrete steps toward giving up their weapons as required by the NPT. Washington maintains that its nuclear capability is essential and has suggested the US is prepared to use nuclear weapons in retaliation for a chemical or biological attack. Other nations hold on to their nuclear weapons for a mix of reasons: Russia and China seek protection against each other and against the US, while France and Britain are apparently seduced by the status of being nuclear powers, since their mini nuclear arsenals are superfluous in theory, given the protective umbrella of NATO ally America. Israel, India and Pakistan also hold fast, justifying their programs for defense against regional enemies.[37]

The Bush Administration has virtually abandoned the international disarmament effort as the world has known it for half a century. Washington not only seeks to further its own nuclear weapons development, but it has also reinterpreted the NPT to deny the relative importance of obligations to eliminate nuclear weapons over time. Washington has argued that the problem is not the existence of weapons, but who controls the finger on the launch buttons. It is an approach that shifts the focus from universal solutions to divisive head-to-head confrontations. And that in turn not only exacerbates the general tensions between haves and have-nots, but also diminishes chances of success by reinforcing the national pride and determination of a country like Iran. Moreover, Washington's 2007 agreement on peaceful nuclear cooperation with India in effect caved in to Delhi's insistence that it too needs nuclear weapons. The bilateral deal, which may well fail to get necessary legislative approvals in either country, simply brushes aside the NPT by neither holding India to the norms of NPT signatories, nor requiring Delhi to sign the NPT as a condition for any US contributions to its nuclear program.

There is an upcoming opportunity to close NPT loopholes and bolster enforcement capability—the Treaty comes up for a major review by all signatories in 2010, and talks to set the agenda have been underway for several years. The Preparatory Committee meetings have been hamstrung, however, by the continuing antagonisms between the haves and have-nots, the revisionist approach of the Bush Administration, and Iran's efforts to evade even the hint of criticism for its nuclear program. The Committee session in 2005 ended in disarray, and the one in 2007 barely managed to keep the process alive.

Looking to the NPT meeting in 2010, governments of most western democracies and experts at think tanks like the Carnegie Endowment have urged a range of steps to strengthen the nonproliferation regime. Top priority proposals from such quarters include agreements to halt the production of fissile material for weapons use, prevent construction of new reprocessing and enrichment facilities in non-nuclear states and assure strictly controlled fuel services for nuclear power plants. The Bush Administration has obstinately resisted moves in these directions—notwithstanding an unusual push from four distinguished American statesmen—Henry Kissinger, George Shultz, Sam Nunn and William Perry—who called in January 2007 for American leadership to realize "the promise of the NPT" and work for "a world free of nuclear weapons."[38]

The other WMDs—what about anthrax and sarin?

Proliferation of non-nuclear WMDs could cost thousands of innocent lives in the hands of an unprincipled dictator or a terrorist group. A March 1995 attack by a Japanese religious cult using the chemical nerve gas sarin in Tokyo's subways, though luckily killing 'only' 12 people, illustrated the horrors that could occur, especially in large cities. The anthrax scares in the US led to few fatalities, but attested to the potential killing power of biological weapons. Osama Bin Laden's wealth and the reach of his network heightens fears that Al Qaeda or some other terrorist organization could acquire non-nuclear WMDs despite the existence of conventions barring both chemical and biological weapons.

The Chemical Weapons Convention is generally acknowledged to be reasonably effective with its comprehensive enforcement regime and the broad coverage of 182 signatory states. The signatories cannot simply rest on their laurels, however, since of the seven states that have not signed as of mid-2007, North Korea and Syria are suspected to possess weapons, and others who have signed may not have declared their stocks for destruction. As for terrorists, it is not easy to obtain many of the most dangerous chemicals, but neither are controls airtight given that some governments resist intrusive inspections and dual-use substances are hard to regulate in any case.

The Biological Weapons Convention, in sharp contrast to the CWC, imposes no obligations on signatories to declare programs or stocks, nor does it have any international enforcement mechanism. Negotiations to address these shortcomings were suspended in 2001 after the Bush Administration declined to participate in further drafting on grounds that any results would be ineffective and too burdensome for the American pharmaceutical industry. It is true that some biological weapons can be made easily and cheaply, and some are very difficult to control in the best of circumstances, but allowing the weaknesses of the BWC to persist makes life much easier for those states and non-state actors who aspire to acquire them.

Landmines and small arms—NGOs into the breach

Ordinary citizens took up the cudgels when major powers hedged on eliminating landmines, which have caused death and dreadful injuries to innocents in post-conflict areas. A 1996 CD protocol to strengthen the 1980 Conventional Weapons Convention did not go far enough for activists who wanted a complete ban on both production and use of anti-personnel land mines. A grass roots NGO campaign swung into action in 1996 and struck a chord with the public. An unprecedented effort led by the International Campaign to Ban Landmines (ICBL) persuaded the Norwegian Government to host negotiations in Oslo. A comprehensive treaty was agreed, and at the end of 1997 was signed in Ottawa by 122 governments (33 more had joined in by August 2007). The ICBL and its coordinator, Jody Williams, received the Nobel Peace Prize for their work.

The landmine treaty's implementation has been uncommonly effective. Although the US, China, Russia, India, Pakistan and the two Koreas have not signed on, most observe the treaty in part. Many minefields have been cleared, large stockpiles of mines have been destroyed, and production and transfers are down dramatically. The UN established a Mine Action Service (UNMAS) to coordinate all aspects of mine action within the UN system and provide field assistance for peacekeeping and humanitarian operations. The Bush Administration has supported several mine clearance projects, but in February 2004 backed away from its predecessor's declaration of intent to join the treaty; it issued a new policy that permits the use of self-destructing mines indefinitely and extends a special exception for Korea.

NGOs have also been prodding governments for more controls on the illegal trade of small arms and light weapons (SA/LW or SALW), categories that include grenades, assault rifles, and shoulder-fired missiles. It is clear that the ready availability of such arms contributes to high levels of violence in areas of conflict or repression. In July 2001, the UN held a major conference to address the subject, followed in July 2003 by the first Biennial Meeting of States to work on the plan of action. But progress on the SALW initiative has been difficult and slow. Many governments are unwilling or unable to contribute full information to the UN's Register of Conventional Arms, and in the US, pro-gun lobbies have mobilized successfully to inhibit legislative action, as when the US Senate in June 2004 failed to act on a convention negotiated by the Organization of American States to track illicit sales and shipments.

In December 2006, the General Assembly approved a resolution calling for an arms trade treaty to establish standards for the import, export and transfer of conventional arms. Aimed to reduce the flow of arms that nurture civil wars as well as to make acquisition more difficult for criminals and terrorists, the proposal passed with 153 affirmative votes, 24 abstentions and one "no" from the Bush Administration. The American pro-gun lobby, the National Rifle Association, pressed Washington for its negative vote and denounced any such agreement. On the other side, a large number of NGOs, Western European governments and countries like Japan, a co-sponsor, pressed forward in 2007 to begin drafting the treaty.

Arms controlling or arms racing—the future of disarmament negotiations

The UN Charter's principled global approach to arms regulation has been stuck at post-Cold War plateaus reached in the 1990s. The Bush neocon alternative, stressing America's overwhelming military prowess and inviting confrontations with perceived enemies, has exacerbated divisions and asphyxiated several promising negotiations for strengthening WMD controls. As the President of the Carnegie Endowment for Peace, Jessica Tuchman Matthews, put it, Washington under Bush "has set a course of ending the United States' traditional leadership in the pursuit of arms control."[39]

Others share the blame for derailing disarmament. Russia and EU countries sold enough arms between them to account for 50% of global exports in 2006 according to SIPRI surveys, which also found that overall arms exports jumped 50% from 2002 to 2006. China's increasing defense budgets concern many, although Beijing still spends less than 10% of the US level, even after Iraq war costs are taken out of the comparison. And too many NAM countries still act irresponsibly in multilateral forums by coddling governments that refuse to sign on to disarmament treaties or prevent meaningful compliance inspections.

The issue is how to move from where the world is now to a more secure place. There are promising agendas for multilateral negotiations in WMD forums, and opportunities continue knocking at the UN door for other arms control steps from small arms to outer space systems. No major advances are likely—or possible—in any of these venues, however, without catalyzing leadership, and the only potential candidate for that role is the US Administration that will take office in January 2009.

PART III

To Reaffirm Faith in Fundamental Human Rights

8

Declarations and Implementation—Standards and Double Standards[40]

○ ○

"Sixty years ago, representatives from 16 nations gathered to begin deliberations on a new international bill of rights. The document they produced is called the Universal Declaration of Human Rights—and it stands as a landmark achievement in the history of human liberty. It opens by recognizing "the inherent dignity" and the "equal and inalienable rights of all members of the human family" as "the foundation of freedom, justice, and peace in the world." And as we gather for this 62nd General Assembly, the standards of the Declaration must guide our work in this world."

—President George W. Bush, UN General Assembly, September 2007

Faith in fundamental human rights was the second of the UN's founding principles after the elimination of war. Accepting the Nobel Peace Prize in 2001 as UN Secretary General, Kofi Annan expressed belief that the UN in the twenty-first century would be defined by "a new, more profound awareness of the sanctity and dignity of every human life, regardless of race or religion."

Indeed, progress on human rights depends heavily on the UN's periodic global convocations, the work of its High Commissioner for Human Rights, special investigations and rapporteurs. But the UN's main forum, the Human Rights

Council, continues to disgrace itself by ignoring gross violations and pampering governments numbered among the worst violators.

Americans champion human rights and have led the way in formulating declarations and setting high standards. In 2007, however, many Americans cannot reconcile their President's high-blown rhetoric with his policies that run counter to the mainstream human rights movement, and seem even to condone torture. This chapter examines the status of world-wide efforts to advance human rights, and considers why NGOs, not Washington officials, carry the American flag into the fray.

The Universal Declaration of Human Rights—the standards are set

The Universal Declaration on Human Rights sets the global standard. Adopted by the General Assembly on December 10, 1948, it identifies the will of the people as the basis of government authority, thus implicitly underwriting democracy as the UN's approved system of government. The Declaration emphasizes groups of inalienable rights relating to every person's life, liberty, and security—rights not to be tortured and not to be arbitrarily arrested or exiled. It also covers rights to safety and mobility, participation in politics, government, and community life, and economic, social, and cultural rights. Importantly, it proposes as well that when individuals' rights are infringed, the world community has a right and an obligation to intervene. But the universality of human rights collides with the right of sovereign states to non-interference in their domestic jurisdiction—put another way, the right to protect victims could be used to justify armed intervention, while the right of non-interference could be used to permit human rights abuse.

The Declaration provides only ambiguously for implementation. US Ambassador Jeane Kirkpatrick once called it "a letter to Santa Claus."[41] Few of the member states that adopted it in 1948 could honestly say that they didn't discriminate against any of their own citizens on the basis or race, sex, religion, political opinion, social origin, property, birth "or other status," or that everyone in their countries had equal protection of the law, or was never subject to arbitrary arrest, detention or exile, or could not be found guilty for an act that was not an offense when it was committed. Indeed, few of them can truthfully say so now.

Many UN members, for example, regularly deny the right to asylum; some allow marriage to occur without the free consent of spouses; some prohibit women from owning property; some limit freedom of thought, conscience, religion, opinion and expression, peaceful assembly, and membership of associations. The rights to participate in "periodic and genuine" elections, to receive equal pay, to join trade unions, to have adequate time off from work, and even to work and be paid, are circumscribed in some countries. The right to education may exist in principle but for the poor in many countries, it is severely limited in practice.

Responsibility to Protect—filling the void?

Almost as an afterthought, the drafters of the Universal Declaration—perhaps exhausted—added a brief mention of duties to their long catalogue of rights. Every man, they said in Article 29, has duties to the community "in which alone the free and full development of his personality is possible," but they failed to specify what those duties were.

The mass killings in Bosnia and Rwanda caused UN members to consider anew the responsibility of states to protect endangered people. An independent body established by the Canadian government in September 2000, the International Commission on Intervention and State Sovereignty (ICISS), gathered experts to work out better ways to respond to man-made crises that threatened large-scale loss of life. The Commission's report was released in December 2001, titled the Responsibility to Protect (R2P).

The R2P report produced a new way of talking about humanitarian intervention and sovereignty. The central theme, in the words of the ICISS website,[42] is "the idea that sovereign states have a responsibility to protect their own citizens from avoidable catastrophe, but that when they are unwilling or unable to do so, that responsibility must be borne by the broader community of states." The report argued the responsibility to protect cannot be conditional and must be universal. As mentioned in Chapter 4 above, the main R2P concept was folded into the Declaration endorsed by world leaders at the 2005 UN Summit in New York, but as with the Universal Declaration, governments generally ignore the implications of their commitment whenever it suits them.

The human rights system—long on process

The Charter and the Declaration call on the UN human rights system to deal with inhumanity of many kinds in many places. But the system's enforcement mechanism was weak—unwieldy bodies charged to monitor adherence to the existing declarations and treaties. Two were set up under the Charter and five under later treaties.[43] While the whole is all too often preoccupied with process, the last three decades have achieved the introduction of an individual complaints system, the appointment of High Commissioners, and the acceptance by states, however grudgingly, of external scrutiny of their human rights records.

Four High Commissioners for Human Rights have been appointed by the Secretary General since the post was first authorized at the Vienna Conference on Human Rights in 1993. Although they have only limited investigative powers, the high-profile men and women of different nationalities appointed to the job have traveled widely, seeking to work with NGOs, academic institutions, and the private sector at national, regional, and international levels. To some extent, they have given a voice to victims, and moral authority to the UN's decisions.

Rapporteurs and special envoys are actively looking into human rights shortfalls on the major themes of UN interest from rights of the girl child to torture. It is not all just spinning wheels—in reaction to the armed repression of dissent by the military junta in Myanmar in mid-2007, a UN Special Envoy carried the message of international concern to the generals, and even the disjointed Human Rights Council moved itself to consider action.

The Human Rights Council (HRC) itself has been turned into something of a bad joke by the UN's member states which determine its composition. Some of the world's worst abusers of human rights have been elected to membership, and even to the chair. The HRC has routinely ignored even the most obvious violations, but continued to bash Israel, while governments like those of China, Libya, Saudi Arabia, Zimbabwe, and numerous others use positions on the Council to deflect criticism of their own behavior. The Bush Administration has refused to stand for membership on the Council, although some NGOs urge it to seek election in order to work for improvement from the inside.

Aside from the HRC, the UN human rights system has been badly served by member states in other ways as well. The Office of the High Commissioner for Human Rights is under-resourced, depending on voluntary contributions by member states for two thirds of its budget. Special Rapporteurs and Representatives are often underpaid and short-staffed. The Charter bodies and the Treaty bodies alike are inefficient and cumbersome, and they produce reports that one observer charitably described as being of "variable quality."[44] Governments either oppose or circumvent the complaints system when it applies to them. Even the advanced democracies, such as the US and Australia, peevishly reject UN reports that venture words of criticism on their practices.

If nothing else, the array of UN forums is available to NGOs working hard to expose human rights violations and press for redress. Among them, the International Committee of the Red Cross makes careful, confidential reports to governments on the treatment of prisoners; Amnesty International and Human Rights Watch expose human rights abuses in many countries; International PEN supports imprisoned writers and journalists; and the International Crisis Group is active in numerous trouble spots, collecting and disseminating evidence on conflict and potential conflict. The Internet has added exponentially to the effectiveness of these western NGOs, which are gradually being joined by others in Latin America and Asia.

Also on the positive side, international courts are slowly grinding out advances in human rights. The International Criminal Tribunals to try those accused of genocide in Rwanda and Bosnia are taking their deliberate course; one for Sierra Leone has started work and another for Cambodia is on the verge. The International Criminal Court has active investigations underway involving Uganda, the Democratic Republic of the Congo, the Central African Republic and Sudan (Darfur). The International Court of Justice has ruled that Israel's "security fence" violates international law and must be dismantled—although its decision is not binding. The ICJ also found that Uganda must pay reparations for its cross-border plundering in the DRC, the amount of which in 2007 was under active negotiation between the two governments.

Of several sites where the supporters and opponents of international law on human rights often clash, or divide, or collide, we will briefly consider genocide and torture. Each is an area in which the UN has an opportunity to do something that member states, whether acting alone or in groups, cannot do: achieve universally agreed definitions of these crimes, work towards an understanding of their causes, and take legitimate action against them.

Genocide—never again means exactly what?

"Never again," the world said after the Holocaust—but genocide has happened again ... and again. The Genocide Convention of 1948 (Convention on the Prevention and Punishment of the Crime of Genocide) stated that in peace or war, genocide—acting with "intent to destroy" a whole population or ethnic group—is a crime under international law that parties to the Convention have a duty to prevent and punish. When genocide did occur, however, the Perm-5 and other powerful UN member states rationalized away their responsibilities to intervene or delayed until too late—as in Cambodia, Bosnia, Rwanda, and Darfur.

As of 2007, member states have generally come to accept that the non-intervention principle is overridden when ethnic cleansing and human rights violations occur on a large scale. The question of just what constitutes genocide under the Convention, however, has tied the UN up in knots on several occasions. The Convention's intent was to head off another Holocaust, but by stating that genocide must be *planned and deliberate*, it created a kind of trap. A state that plans to commit genocide won't admit it, so an investigating commission of other states must be set up to establish guilt—a time-consuming process that inevitably allows more people to die.

Annan's High Level Panel in 2004 had no easy answers to the questions of planning, urgency, and scale of genocide. Citing the "emerging norm" of the R2P principle, the High Level Panel urged that it should apply to all serious instances of avoidable human catastrophe—mass murder and rape, ethnic cleansing by forcible expulsion and terror, and deliberate starvation and exposure to disease—and that the Security Council should, as a last resort, authorize force to deal with it. But the political will still failed to materialize for Darfur.

Darfur—crime in progress, 2003 to ...?

The black African Muslims of Darfur, an arid region about the size of Iraq with some 80 tribes, had for long found themselves excluded from the power and benefits Khartoum received from the oil-rich parts of their territory. In 2003, Darfuri rebel groups rose against the government, and Khartoum in addition to using its own forces, recruited armed nomad militiamen, the Janjaweed Arabs, to put down the revolt. Defying the Security Council's call in July for an end to the killing within a month, Khartoum continued to fly military aircraft into Darfur, and support the Janjaweed pillaging. Sudanese President Omar Bashir claimed the West's motive was the same as in Iraq—to grab Sudan's oil and gold.

Fighting continued to escalate. By May 2004, more than one million Darfuris were displaced; by August, ethnic cleansing had driven over 100,000 into neighboring Chad; and up to 10,000 people were dying each month. The Janjaweed were reliably reported to be committing murder, rape and arson, to the extent that in September 2004, US Secretary of State Colin Powell called it genocide. But no effective action followed to rein in Khartoum and the Janjaweed.

The Security Council's inquiry on Darfur took three months and then opined in early 2005 that there had been "crimes against humanity," but not genocide in the narrow, post-World War II definition that required proof of intent to destroy a population group. The Secretary General urged that those accused of crimes against humanity should be brought before the International Criminal Court. The US, which does not recognize the ICC, opposed this, proposing instead a specific war crimes tribunal to be held in Tanzania. But in April 2005, the US abstained on a vote in the Security Council, thus clearing the way for Sudanese war criminals to be prosecuted in the ICC, on the condition that no Americans working in Sudan were subject to its jurisdiction.

How could the killing be stopped and the accused be arrested? The African Union began to deploy a protective force (the African Mission in Sudan—AMIS) in August 2004, building to a strength of 7,000 by mid-2005, but it was ill-equipped and far too small for the job. Finally, after much posturing and half-hearted threats from the Security Council, the US and the EU, Khartoum in mid-2006 reluctantly agreed in principle to accept an international contingent of UN troops to supplement AMIS.

Darfuri suffering continued unchecked into 2007. Well over 2 million people were homeless and somewhere over 200,000 (some defend estimates over 400,000) had probably died from fighting and privation. But the Security Council continued to hold back as members protected the narrow interests mentioned earlier—China's oil imports from Sudan, Russia's arms sales to Khartoum, US anti-terrorist concerns and other regional interests, and a host of countries unwillingness to challenge Arab unity with Sudanese leaders. At the UN General Assembly in September 2007, representatives of nearly 30 countries and regional bodies talked about speeding up a 26,000-strong joint AU-UN force for Darfur, but deployment was conditioned on arrangements with a reluctant Khartoum, and little changed on the ground as the hybrid force's take-over was delayed until January 2008 at the earliest.

Darfur thus proved yet another object lesson on how easily principles are agreed upon, and how difficult they are to put into practice. UN envoys and the Secretary General pricked the world's conscience; UN agencies and NGOs delivered aid to the refugees; the Security Council badgered Khartoum; and the African Union sent a token military force. But member states failed to take decisive action, and Sudan sat on the UN Commission for Human Rights for much of the time that the tragedy unfolded.

Torture—plain or compassionate

Compared to more complex concepts like "human rights," and "terrorism," the meaning of "torture" is widely understood and accepted. Or it was until the Bush Administration in 2003, after inventing new categories of persons to whom the Geneva Conventions did not apply, redefined permissible techniques for extracting information from them.

Soon after 9/11, US forces in Afghanistan and American agents elsewhere rounded up hundreds suspected of being terrorists or having links to Al Qaeda. To legitimize the process, Washington created a new category for them, "enemy combatant," that appears nowhere in the four Geneva Conventions, the universally agreed standard for treatment of non-combatants and prisoners of war. On November 13, 2001, Bush issued an order for the "detention, treatment and trial of certain non-citizens in the war against terrorism," providing exemptions to the Conventions.[45] Then, in a notorious memo, Assistant Attorney-General Jay Bybee advised the President's legal counsel in August 2002 that "cruel, inhuman, or degrading treatment" of these prisoners could be reclassified as "not torture." Rather, the memo averred, torture was pain that came with "serious physical injury such as organ failure, impairment of body function or even death." Moreover, US laws against torture did not apply "to detentions and interrogations of enemy combatants pursuant to the President's Commander in Chief authority."

The graphic revelations of degrading treatment meted out to prisoners at Abu Ghraib and elsewhere were followed by stories of "extraordinary renditions." This practice of sending suspects to countries other than the US for interrogation was also known to have occurred under President Clinton, but at that time it required White House approval and had follow-up measures intended to preclude torture.

Under Bush, rendition with fewer controls was reportedly carried out in Egypt, Indonesia, Jordan, Libya, Morocco, Pakistan, and Uzbekistan—hooded and handcuffed passengers were put on board and taken to some of those countries, where authorities were merely "asked not to torture them."[46]

Allegations of torture also emerged from the detention center at Guantanamo Bay in Cuba, which the White House claimed was outside US jurisdiction. But in June 2004, the US Supreme Court ruled that it had the jurisdiction to entertain petitions from detainees. Further, the Court in October 2004 considered the human rights of the 550 detainees from 42 countries held at Guantanamo Bay, and found that "a state of war is not a blank check for the President" to detain people indefinitely without just cause. The US began releasing and repatriating them, before the military commission had heard their cases, but without laying charges or offering apologies or compensation. In January 2005, the *New England Journal of Medicine* reported that US army doctors had violated medical ethics and the Geneva Conventions by taking part in "abusive interrogations" at detention camps. In March 2005, American human rights lawyers filed a suit against Donald Rumsfeld on behalf of eight men they said were tortured by US forces in custody in Iraq and Afghanistan, but the case was dismissed two years later, indicating the chances of those ultimately responsible appearing before a court are slight.

Prospects

Governments acting through the UN could obviously do far more to defend human rights. For starters, member states could elect only governments with acceptable human rights records to key UN bodies working on human rights issues, above all the Human Rights Council. A more competent Council with a more qualified membership could intervene to defend or restore elected governments, and be less selective in its approach to countries that commit human rights violations. Member states could also press for stronger measures to implement the Responsibility to Protect principles and follow-up on their commitments in the Vienna Declaration and Plan of Action of 1993, which explicitly linked democracy, development, and respect for human rights—this applies especially to the more than 100 democratic countries which signed a similar pledge, the Warsaw Declaration, in June 2000.

The divisions that haunt the UN apply to human rights as well. Although the Universal Declaration has been accepted by all, major cultural and religious differences are evident throughout the world in norms for treatment of women, family, property rights and so on. China has led those in Asia who argue that the right of the community to economic advancement overrides the right of the individual to liberty. Even leaders of nominal democracies like Singapore have put their view that too much democracy is a bad thing into practice, prosecuting opposition leaders to the point of bankruptcy, hanging drug smugglers, and outlawing homosexuality.

Nor, obviously, is the West accepted by all as a model just because it is prosperous. Others point to the excessive definition of freedom in the West where, as they see it, families do not take responsibility for the aged and ill, and the state does not give due assistance for health care, education, or employment. Some from authoritarian traditions have argued that the well-being of the nation is a long-term matter, not something to be bargained away every three or four years by politicians facing elections. With regard to human rights, there is a clash of cultures, if not of civilizations, which needs to be confronted, better understood and resolved.

Where is America in this picture? A US Senator stung by criticism of Washington's recent record thundered in response that no country had done as much for human rights as America. But it is not what America has done in the past that counts—it is what America is doing now. In 2007, the government in Washington continued to violate fundamental human rights in its quest to vanquish terrorists, to infringe fundamental freedoms of its own citizens in the guise of defending the homeland, and to scorn international law as an impediment to its own freedom of action. These excesses have overshadowed official US interventions to promote human rights. Washington's credibility on human rights verges on non-existent.

9

Women and Children—Unkept Promises

o o o o o o o o o o o o o o o o o o o o o o o o o o o o o o o o o o o
Governments worldwide have adopted a piecemeal and incremental approach to implementation that cannot achieve the economic, social and political transformation underlying the promises and vision of Beijing.

—*Women's Environment and Development Organization (WEDO) 2005*[47]

UN documents have set modern global standards for the rights of women and children. There is no lack of advocacy by civil society or of UN machinery for the advancement of women and girls and for the protection of the rights of children.

The 1995 UN Fourth World Conference on Women in Beijing jolted many governments into action and brought a measure of progress. Yet, a culture of discrimination persists, some states blatantly deny equal rights to women, and even in advanced democracies, men retain a disproportionate share of political and economic power. As for children, there have been gains in school attendance and health, but goals are still unmet and in much of the world there are few mechanisms to save them from exploitation.

Why haven't the declarations and plans of action produced more results? And where is America in the campaign to advance the causes of women and children, given that the US Senate (almost alone among western democracies) refuses to ratify the fundamental treaties?

The following sections consider the status of efforts to realize the promises made on paper to women and children.

Women's rights are human rights—in principle[48]

Women have for centuries demanded equality—with varying success. It has even been said by some that women have it, but such assertions are unmatched by reality. They have been promised it, particularly at times of war and revolution when their support of the national effort was suddenly seen as indispensable, but it was often snatched away afterwards. The UN Charter and the Universal Declaration of Human Rights gave fresh impetus to women's struggle by asserting the principle of equality between the sexes.

Building on this start, the Convention for the Elimination of All Forms of Discrimination Against Women (CEDAW) in 1979 restated the equal rights and dignity of women and men. It requires signatory states to bring their legislation into conformity with this principle, to establish mechanisms to end discrimination, and to report on compliance every four years to the CEDAW committee of experts. The US is the only industrialized country that has not ratified CEDAW—conservatives in the US Senate have blocked it, objecting in principle to the idea of America's being required to submit a report to outsiders on such a topic.

Ratified by 185 states, CEDAW has been used successfully to advance the status of women by catalyzing programs such a campaign promoting girls' literacy in Egypt and one against domestic violence in Uganda. It has also been backed up by related UN declarations: on the Elimination of Intolerance and of Discrimination Based on Religion or Belief; on the Right to Development; on the Elimination of Violence Against Women; and on other aspects of human rights. The penning of so many words is testimony to recalcitrance around the world in delivering rights to women and girls.

Seeking to go from words to action, a series of international women's conferences led to the benchmark Fourth World Conference on Women in Beijing in 1995. Delegates reaffirmed earlier goals, assessed progress, and succinctly declared, "Women's rights are human rights." The Conference endorsed the Platform for Action, calling for the inclusion of a gender perspective in all policies and programs of member states, along with a plan to achieve by 2000 goals that had been set in the Nairobi Conference of 1985. Over the past decade since Beijing, progress was made in some countries and some regions, and the conditions of many women's lives in the rich countries improved markedly, but the poorest women in the poorest countries have progressed the least, in some ways hardly at all.

Halting progress

There is good news on some fronts. Micro-credit programs are helping women around the world raise their incomes, penny by penny; the Security Council has begun to aggressively promote participation of women in peacekeeping and peacebuilding programs; UNICEF has refocused its programs to emphasize that "gender equality and the well-being of children go hand in hand;" and many governments, in response to CEDAW injunctions, have put laws on the books where none existed before, for example against domestic violence. In Africa, the Protocol on the Rights of Women entered into force in 2005, and as of 2007 has 21 ratifications.

But even now, many states simply ignore their written undertakings. Six decades after the UN Charter, more than five after the Universal Declaration on Human Rights, a quarter century after the CEDAW Convention entered into force, and 12 years after Beijing, too many women are still trafficked, prostituted, impoverished and illiterate, secluded in some countries, virtually enslaved in others. By 2005, women's employment in the non-agricultural sector in developing countries had slowly grown, except in North Africa, where there had been no progress for 15 years. And in most Western countries women still earn less than men and hold less powerful positions.

World-wide, as of August 2007, a new high was reached with 35 women as presiding officers in their parliaments, but the number of heads of state or government who were women totaled only 11, representing no perceptible change in a decade. Women in Kuwait finally gained political rights in 2005, in the face of determined opposition from Islamic representatives. The publicity that greeted their achievement, and the election of women to 23% of seats in the United Arab Emirates Parliament in 2006, reminded the world that participation was still denied to many others, and that the countries where women hold more than a third of seats in parliaments could be numbered on two hands.

Millennium Development Goal 3 aims to promote gender equality and empower women.[49] By 2007, modest progress had been made. As measured by the number of girls enrolled in primary school, most regions had progressed, with 88% of primary school age children enrolled overall. But girls still lagged behind boys, and of the 72 million children not in school in 2005, 57% were girls. No data were available from 'conflict sites.' MDG 4 targets preventable deaths of children under five and MDG 5 seeks to reduce maternal mortality—the data in 2007 showed tragically high mortality rates in sub-Saharan Africa and South Asia. In sub-Saharan Africa, one in 16 women was at risk of dying from treatable complications in pregnancy or childbirth, while in the developed world the risk was one in 3,800.

The 1995 Beijing conference asserted that the "explicit recognition and reaffirmation of the right of all women to control all aspects of their health, in particular their own fertility, is basic to their empowerment." But a decade later, women's confidence in claiming such control had somewhat deflated by continuing pressures from the persistence of religious fundamentalism, the spread of conflict, and the consequences of patchy economic conditions. The Bush Administration has increased contributions to Africa for AIDS, worked to liberate Afghan women at least in the Kabul area, and supported programs aimed at preventing trafficking, rape, sexual exploitation, and domestic violence. But on two related issues affecting women, prostitution and abortion, the Administration appeared to have moved back more than a decade. Its efforts to restrict women's access to abortions, not only in America but also in other countries, particularly in China, were met with outrage at the 2005 UN women's meeting in New York.

The crush of poverty, patriarchal traditions and disempowerment leaves women and children particularly vulnerable to sexual abuse and exploitation. Here, we look briefly at sex crimes against women and children, and the pernicious impact of HIV/AIDS.

Crimes against women and children—sex and slavery

"Honor killings," revenge rape, rape within marriage, and other violations of women's rights continue, often justified as "cultural" and "preserving tradition." Honor killings are unlawful in most countries in the Middle East and South Asia, but, for example, an estimated 80 Palestinian women and girls are killed each year, often by their families, for as little as making contact with a male who is not a relative. The killers are rarely arrested or prosecuted. In Afghanistan, where much has been made of the transition to democracy, a woman in her 20s was publicly stoned to death for adultery in May 2005. Revenge rape by men of one family against a woman of another is not uncommon, and laws requiring evidence from several male witnesses of a rape are weighted against the victim.

The UN's members often take a selective approach to human rights, especially the rights of women. Majorities in the UN human rights system and the General Assembly overlook the human rights implications of many cultural and religious traditions that disadvantage women. Little has been said, for example, about the extreme gender discrimination practiced in Saudi Arabia. The UN did criticize Iran in December 2004 for public executions, torture, arbitrary sentencing, flogging, stoning, and discrimination against women, although that only came after Iran was in the Security Council's sights because of its nuclear ambitions.

The UN chose 2004 as its year to commemorate the struggle against slavery. Outlawed in the 19th century, slavery has changed its form and methods. Being a bonded laborer is slavery, and that persists, particularly in South Asia and parts of Africa. Trafficking in men, women and children is equivalent to slavery, when they are forced to work against their will, as still happens in many countries. The ILO estimates that 179 million children aged between five and 17 are child laborers, and many live in virtual is slavery, as do untold numbers of women and girls, who are forced into marriage. Being a child soldier can also be slavery, and girls who are forced to be "soldiers' wives" are sex slaves as well.

Prostitution in the case of poor women everywhere has always been a way to make more money of their own than they could in other low-paid industries. Michael Maren argued in *The Road to Hell* (1997) that men (and women, he might have added) who encourage child prostitution are criminals, but an African woman who freely chooses to go into prostitution is making a rational decision, to make real money, under conditions usually better than working on a farm or in a sweatshop factory, and with not much more risk to her health. Similar decisions are made by young women everywhere, but particularly in rural communities in Latin and Central America and South, Southeast, and East Asia. In 2005, the US Government put the contrary argument that the way to curb the trafficking of women and sex tourism was to ban prostitution. Since this would be likely to drive all three—prostitution, trafficking, and sex tourism—further underground, women's rights advocates at the UN women's 'Being plus 10' conference in New York resisted it.

HIV/AIDS—stalking women and children

Human rights gains for women are in danger of being lost to HIV/AIDS. In 2004, the annual AIDS update prepared by the UN, WHO, and the World Bank detected that women once thought to be low risk, were being infected far more than in the past. In the Caribbean, young women's risk of infection was twice that of young men. In India, where about 5.1 million people were infected, women accounted for a quarter of new infections. In Papua New Guinea, HIV/AIDS infections were doubling every two years, with girls of 14 to 19 having the highest infection rate, and unfaithful husbands reported to be the major transmitters. The trend was worst in sub-Saharan Africa, where women comprised 57% of people living with the virus. In South Africa, Zambia, and Zimbabwe, women aged 15 to 24 were three to six times more likely to be infected than young men. As one of the few brighter spots, reports from Uganda showed that an 'ABC' program led by the President and his wife urging people to abstain, be faithful, or use a condom was producing encouraging results.

In all regions, the percentage of infected women either increased or stayed the same between 2002 and 2004. For women anywhere, being in monogamous, long-term relationships has been no guarantee of safety.[50] In the US, a 2004 study showed that women in a low-income area of New York were twice as likely to be infected by their husbands or long-term lovers as by a casual partner. Risks that women shared, even in developed countries, included their physical vulnerability, their partners' refusal to use condoms, their husbands' infidelity, the high-risk behavior of other male partners, older men's exploitation of young women, rape, and other forms of sexual coercion, as well as intravenous drug use.

By late 2004, UNAIDS had reached the conclusion that, to check the epidemic, fundamental changes were required in the conditions of life for women and girls. Peter Piot, the Director of UNAIDS, argued that women had to be central to the response. UNFPA advocated programs for women—education, employment, and rights to inherit homes and property. By 2005, more than 1.5 million children were estimated by the UN to have lost one or both parents to AIDS, with consequences for the future that can only be imagined. In 2006, deaths from AIDS had increased to 2.9 million, and UNAIDS admitted that preventive measures were failing to keep pace with the spread of the disease.

Gender equality inside the UN—not what it should be

The UN has a number of agencies to advance the status of women: there is the Commission on the Status of Women; UNIFEM for women in development; INSTRAW for research and training; and OSAGI, the Office of the Special Advisor for Gender Issues and the Advancement of Women, to "strengthen the implementation" of all the promises ticked off above.

If charity begins at home, where does the UN itself stand on implementing gender equality? In August 2007, the Special Advisor, Assistant Secretary General Rachel Mayanja, reported, "In the United Nations system itself, progress on women's representation has been limited and uneven and the goal of reaching 50/50 gender balance remains elusive. As of December 31, 2005 in the larger group of Professional Staff with appointments of one year or more, the representation of women stood at 37.7% with a slight improvement from the previous year. At the senior levels (D-1 and above), it is 24%. None of the current peace operations is headed by a woman."[51] The advances from the inequalities of 50 years ago may be applauded, but the dismaying picture of stalled progress raises anew the challenges of when and how to give women their full due.

Sexual harassment has also been an issue in UN hallways. Allegations of improper behavior led to the resignation (with no admission of guilt) in early 2005 of the UN High Commission for Refugees, and there have been other cases. To his credit, Kofi Annan took a strong stand while he was Secretary General and internal procedures in place as of mid-2007 seem on par with western governmental standards, at least on paper.

Far more shocking problems came to light with evidence that sexual abuse of women and children was rife among UN peacekeepers in the Democratic Republic of the Congo. Similar accusations against UN peacekeepers widened the scandal in March 2005, when a UNICEF official implicated servicemen in Burundi, Haiti, Liberia, and Namibia.[52] As described in Chapter 4 above, primary responsibility rested with commanders of contributed forces and with the Security Council which sets the terms of peace operations, but "the UN" inevitably gets the blame in public eyes. Corrective actions have been taken and the burden has now been unambiguously shifted to the Secretariat to ensure aggressive monitoring and swift investigation of reported abuse.

Children—the most vulnerable[53]

International rhetoric is replete with passionate statements on behalf of children. But somewhere on the way from policy to action, the fervor to stop the violation of children's human rights often gets lost, just as it does with the rights of women. For many, the idea of children having rights is new and strange. The Geneva Declaration asserted the principle in 1924, the Universal Declaration of Human Rights identifies childhood as entitled to special assistance, and the UN Declaration of the Rights of the Child (1959) reasserted the need of children for appropriate legal protection "before as well as after birth."

The UN Convention on the Rights of the Child (CRC) of 1989 has been ratified by all member states except the US and Somalia. The treaty, recognizing both the vulnerability of children and primacy of parents, sets forth rights and entitlements that should accrue to children. US Senate conservatives initially blocked ratification because children under 18 were excluded from armed forces (the US military accepts seventeen year-olds), but when that feature was fixed by an Optional Protocol which the US has ratified, right wing activists continued to prevent the treaty's adoption, evidently on principle, distrusting such outside instruments and their possible impact on US traditions.

Children in poor countries face enormous problems and exploitation, even though the CRC has led to some advances on four key concepts: survival, development, protection, and participation. UNICEF in late 2004 reported that the lives of more than one billion children were at risk because of poverty, war, and disease. One in six children, it said, was very hungry, one in seven was denied health care, one in five lacked access to safe water, and one in three had no toilet at home. An estimated 18 million African children will have lost one or both parents to AIDS by 2010. In 2007, UNICEF's annual study, *The State of the World's Children*, showed continued high rates of child labor and marriage in violation of the Convention 15 years after its entry into force. In Chapters 11–13, we will take up the international effort to reduce this level of suffering, in particular through Millennium Development Goals focused on children and mothers.

Trafficking in children

Researchers of trafficking in children have found that its main causes include family poverty, the particular vulnerability of children, social exclusion, and discrimination. Children are trafficked for many purposes—prostitution, labor, servitude, early marriage, illicit adoption (not least by rich world parents), and even for 'harvesting' organs. Young children are needed to knot and weave rugs in several Middle Eastern countries, and boys are still used as jockeys in the United Arab Emirates, in spite of a ban on those under 16. In 2007 a daring journalist in China reported child labor in mines and quarries. A certain degree of global hypocrisy is evident in that many in the developed world take advantage of cheap imports even as they condemn societies where children's work contributes to poor families' income.

UN and NGO reports suggest that children who seek asylum often do so to escape traffickers who may have promised them an escape from persecution in their own country. If they appear to have consented and fail to get refugee status, their fate is either to be returned to the same abusive environment from which they fled, or to be institutionalized in circumstances that further violate their rights. As researcher Sharon Bessell has argued,[54] trafficking has clearly not been stopped by expressions of multilateral will, and therefore a shift to a human rights-based approach may work better, shedding the view of children as victims or beneficiaries of the traders, and regarding them instead as citizens with rights.

Child soldiers—still marching

Of the many plights daily facing children in the developing world, being forced to be soldiers may be the worst violation of their rights. Kofi Annan in 1997 appointed former Ugandan Foreign Minister Olara Otunnu to be a special envoy for the protection of children exposed to armed conflict. A distinguished statesman, Otunnu developed mechanisms for monitoring and reporting on child soldiers, and naming and listing conflicting parties that brutalize children. Notwithstanding his effort, however, Otunnu reported in "Children and Armed Conflict," that children continued to be killed, maimed, raped, abducted and recruited in these local wars.

In 2007, according to UN and NGO estimates, there are about 250,000 child soldiers fighting in armed conflicts in more than 30 countries, some as young as ten, but most between 14 and 18 years old. They include girls, who are at particular risk of rape, sexual harassment, and forced marriage. Child soldiers, defined as those under 18, have been used in front line combat by Burundi, Burma, Congo, and Sudan, and by paramilitary and militia groups in Colombia,

Uganda, and Zimbabwe. Refugees International has found that family poverty impels some two thirds of children to become soldiers. Many children have been abducted, while others, brought up in violent cultures, joined up to prove their "manhood." Aside from service as fighters, some have been used as spies and human shields.

The Optional Protocol to the Convention on the Rights of the Child, which came into force in February 2002, raised the age for direct participation in military forces from 15 to 18, and banned recruitment under 18. Aside from soldiers, the Protocol also covered child pornography, prostitution and trafficking. Most countries moved to ratify it, including the US which worked out language in the document allowing children aged 17 to serve in the American armed forces on condition they be kept from combat. The US has still not signed the Convention itself, however, owing to objections from conservatives that rights of parents might somehow be infringed.

Setting things right

Women face enormous obstacles. UN ASG Mayanja has summarized them as follows: "Critical barriers to women's equal participation in decision-making are deeply rooted in the persistence of stereotypical attitudes on the roles of women—inequitable sharing of family responsibilities between women and men, the absence of enabling environments in political institutions, and women's exclusion from decision-making in critical policy domains, such as international affairs and the economy."

Passive acceptance of gender inequality is pervasive. Most western governments make no bones about doing business with countries where women are not allowed to drive, be educated, work outside their homes, or inherit property, and where divorce laws and penalties for adultery penalize women more severely than men. Many nations passively accept that none of their female diplomats is acceptable as Ambassador to Saudi Arabia, thereby breaching their own principles of equality and non-discrimination as well as those of the UN. Iranian Ambassadors refuse to shake the hands of women diplomats at the UN. The acceptance without demur of this kind of discrimination against more than half of all people, 60 years on, is an indictment of the UN, its agencies, all its members, and the human rights system.

American government leadership could make a big difference. It is hard for others to hold the line when the US refuses to ratify seminal agreements and ties up resources to go its own way rather than join the team. Much of this comes about because of the short-sightedness—virtual paranoia—of American right wing politicians, who fail to see that documents like CEDAW and the Convention on Rights of the Child are no threat to the America, but rather a vehicle to advance the cause of women's and children's rights in countries where women can't begin to dream of attaining the benefits and status enjoyed by those in the US. CEDAW and its Optional Protocol which allows reporting on women's rights direct to the treaty committees, are often the only avenues open for oppressed women to seek relief.

American women have struggled with little success against the smothering influence in the foreign policy realm of archconservatives in the US Senate. It will take a progressive American President, bold Senators and reinvigorated NGO leaders to break out of the rut. In the meantime, the UN system will at least go on doing essential work worldwide that others cannot or will not do, collecting essential global data and measuring progress towards internationally accepted goals for women and children, limited though it seems to be.

10

Refugees and Indigenous Peoples—The Displaced and Disenfranchised

o o o o o o o o o o o o o o o o o o o o o o o o o o o o o o o o o o o o

Say this city has ten million souls,
Some are living in mansions, some are living in holes;
Yet there's no place for us, my dear, yet there's no place for us.

—W.H. Auden, *Refugee Blues*

The number of refugees is on the increase again for the first time since 2002, reaching about 14 million as of mid-2007. The number of internally displaced persons has jumped dramatically, and the count of stateless is up as well. All together, the total of those cast loose on our planet is over 35 million people. Most of them look to the UN as their best, for many their only, hope for protection and sustenance.

Like refugees, many indigenous people find themselves adrift in someone else's culture.

UN involvement with the rights of indigenous people developed much later than its post-war concern with refugees, but both broad groups face similar issues related to the loss of homes or homelands, their rights as displaced or disenfranchised populations, and the limited options available to them.

We look in this chapter at efforts to provide humanitarian assistance, and to sort out rights and responsibilities for dealing with these disadvantaged populations.

Backlash against refugees and migrants complicates the search for humane and durable solutions. What is the outlook?

Refugees[55]—durable problems

What to do about refugees was one of the UN's earliest concerns. Following the displacement through World War II of millions in Europe and Asia, the UN Relief and Works Agency (UNRWA) had a high post-war profile in reconstruction and resettlement. The Office of the UN High Commissioner for Refugees (UNHCR) was created by the UN General Assembly and began work on January 1, 1951 as a temporary agency, expected to be terminated in three years—its mandate has been renewed every five years since 1958.

UNHCR is the most central of numerous UN agencies that help refugees. The High Commissioner is nominated by the Secretary General and elected by the General Assembly. Advice on refugee protection is provided by an Executive Committee of 50 member states, which also oversees the UNHCR budget. With a limited subsidy from the UN budget for administrative expenses, UNHCR's activities are funded by voluntary contributions from governments, NGOs, and individuals, at the rate of more than one billion dollars a year. UNHCR, with 6,000 staff, is one of the biggest UN agencies. Other agencies integrally involved with refugees include the relatively new Office of the Coordinator for Humanitarian Affairs (OCHA), WHO, WFP, UNICEF, and a range of non-UN groups, notably the Red Cross and Red Crescent societies.

Rights and definitions

UNHCR's mission is to ensure that everyone can exercise the right to seek asylum, find safe refuge in another state, and to return home voluntarily. The rights of refugees are set out in the 1951 Convention Relating to the Status of Refugees along with a 1967 Protocol. A refugee, for the UN's purposes, is any person who owing to a well-founded fear of being persecuted for reasons of race, religion, nationality or political opinion, is outside the country of his nationality and is unable or, owing to such fear, is unwilling to avail himself of the protection of that country.

Over the years, this definition of refugees has been widened in practice to include people fleeing from armed conflict, violence, and human rights violations. The

Convention also bars states from penalizing or unnecessarily restricting the movement of refugees who have illegally entered their territory; prohibits expelling refugees on grounds other than national security or public order; and establishes the principle of *non-refoulement*, meaning that no one may be returned against their will to a country where they might be at risk of persecution.

These provisions do not, however, cover what are now called "economic" refugees. A reconsideration is pressing, since it can be virtually impossible to distinguish fairly between those forced to flee for economic or political reasons, and moreover, to do so also raises the human rights principle of the right to paid work. Some refugees from Indochina after the Vietnam War were said not to be fleeing "real" persecution, but seeking economic betterment in countries where they wanted to work illegally or to which they would migrate if they could. Later refugees from China, Afghanistan, and Iraq have been similarly accused. These motivations doubtless drove many as individuals, but they reflect less the overall perfidy of refugees than the desperation of their lives, the ease of global mobility, and their genuine fear of what might happen to them if, having tried illegally to migrate, they are repatriated.

The right of nations to admit or reject anyone seeking to enter their sovereign territory continually collides with the right of *bona fide* refugees and asylum-seekers to protection. Human Rights Watch has found that "in the past 50 years states have largely regressed in their commitment to protect refugees, with the wealthy industrialized states of Europe, North America and Australia ... adopting particularly hostile and restrictive policies ... Since September 11 (2001), many countries have pushed through emergency anti-terrorism legislation that curtails the rights of refugees."[56] The UN's ability to assist refugees and displaced persons becomes ever more curtailed when its members impose self-serving, narrow definitions of who is entitled to help or to admission for resettlement.

Internally Displaced Persons—refugees by another name

Calls have increasingly been made on the UN to help internally displaced persons (IDPs—people forced to move within their own countries) and to extend its services to populations affected by civil war.[57] Such persons are often treated as badly or worse than refugees, a term technically applied only to those who managed to leave their home country. Internal displacement, Kofi Annan wrote in

1998, had emerged as "one of the great human tragedies of our time."[58] In 2004, a SAIS/Brookings report described UN operations in the field on behalf of internally displaced people still to be ad hoc, lacking adequate coordination, money and staff.[59]

By July 2004, Annan had enough support from member states to establish an Inter-Agency Internal Displacement Division within the Office of the Coordinator for Humanitarian Assistance (OCHA). The Division has representation from the major UN agencies involved and NGOs, and a clear mandate to help IDPs. By the end of 2006, almost 13 million such persons were receiving some form of assistance from UNHCR. The suffering of displaced persons in Darfur and Iraq testified anew to the urgency of the problems. Programs and their effectiveness vary widely since what can or can't be done to help IDPs in a target country depends heavily on the attitude and capabilities of that country's government.

Refugees and IDPs pose an enormous problem that keeps mutating wherever violence and vulnerability, mobility and marginalization coincide. Of the 14 million refugees in the world in 2007, many were in countries that could not afford to help them. Another 20 to 25 million were internally displaced, seeking asylum or stateless. In more than 115 countries, the UN provided sustenance and shelter in what began as temporary camps but then became permanent settlements—8.8 million have been "warehoused," confined to camps for ten years or more. Several governments, as indicated by the Human Rights Watch assessment noted above, have sought to stem any inflow into their countries by incarcerating or repatriating people seeking asylum and refugee status, ignoring the legal, moral, and humanitarian aspects of such actions.

"Today's human rights abuses are tomorrow's refugee movements," the UNHCR declared in 1995, adding "the concept of refugee protection is inseparable from the notion of human rights." The UN has been often blamed by both sides for what it had done or not done to protect these rights. Sadako Ogata (2005) records how the UNHCR's relief effort in Bosnia was obstructed: "All parties seemed to believe that our humanitarian assistance fed their 'enemy.'" Guidance sent from the UN to UNHCR staff in the field on how to implement policy was widely ignored, Roberta Cohen, of the Brookings Institution, complained. Male staff in Pakistan, she told us, didn't honor the UN's commitments to equality for women. The small enrollment of Afghan refugee girls in school there was regarded as "cultural" and hence excusable, although the refugee mothers were anxious for their daughters to be educated. What was cultural, Cohen said, was the attitude of some male UN agency staff. The UNHCR did nothing to help refugees fleeing North Korea, Claudia Rosett alleged in the *Wall Street Journal.*[60] But the UNHCR has more than 5,000 staff in the field, and these complaints have to be assessed with perspective on the dedication of the great majority of UNHCR workers to their difficult and often dangerous tasks.

The High Level Panel in 2004 recommended changes to modernize the refugee machinery of the UN, but it stopped short of changing the definition of refugees, or saying more explicitly where responsibility lies for caring and paying for them. While these ambiguities continue, the UNHCR has important work to do in mediating between applicants for asylum and governments that don't want them, collecting and verifying information, and assessing their claims. Strategies now being used by UNHCR include trying to avert movements of people by improving their security in their home countries, and strengthening their ability to return there in safety. Experts are now also struggling to anticipate the impact of climate change on movements of people—sea level rise is already affecting small island populations in the Indian and Pacific Oceans and crop failure, droughts, and floods threaten to make some areas unlivable.

Promising new efforts to improve the delivery of assistance and protection are underway. The Inter-Agency Standing Committee (IASC), the primary mechanism for inter-agency coordination of humanitarian assistance, took measures in 2006 to significantly strengthen performance in the field. The Committee, a unique forum involving the key UN and non-UN humanitarian partners, achieved agreement on a global "cluster approach," which delineates lead agencies and responsibilities for nine activity areas. UNHCR, for example, has the lead for Camp Management; UNICEF for nutrition; UNDP for early recovery; and so on. The IASC has also issued a gender handbook, set forth guidelines for human rights, and established a framework for improving security coordination among IGOs, NGOs and the UN.

Palestinians—58 years and counting

No situation better illustrates the enormous inherent difficulty of resolving a refugee crisis than that of the over 4 million Palestinians, who comprise over one quarter of the world's refugee population. Most are the responsibility of UNRWA, not UNHCR, so they are not counted in UNHCR's statistics on its own activities.

UNRWA was established in 1949 to protect the Palestinian refugees, and to ensure that they returned to their territory or received compensation. UNRWA is still there, and Israel, which accepted these conditions when it joined the UN in 1949, has never implemented them. UNRWA has grown over the years into a huge operation with 25,000 mostly Palestinian employees, and is an important part of the local economy.

UNRWA is caught between its Palestinian clients and the Israelis, who accuse it of not being neutral. The Israelis make life difficult for its staff, who, they say, include Hamas and Hezbollah sympathizers. The schools run by UNRWA are accused by Israel of using Palestinian textbooks that preach incitement to violence. Since 2001 Israel has arrested some 20 of UNRWA's workers, accusing some of using their UN vehicles to transport Palestinian militants. Israelis justify their tough attitude on grounds that an influx of Palestinians seeking a homeland would destroy the Jewish character of Israel.

For their part, Palestinians cite numerous UN resolutions in support of their claims that refugees should be allowed to return to their native land, that Israel should stop destroying the homes of suspected terrorists, and that the Israeli military should withdraw from the territories occupied since the 1967 war. These UN decisions have been ignored by the US and Israel, enraging many Arabs who compare America's inaction on Israel with its decisive operations to punish Sadddam Hussein for defying Security Council resolutions.[61] But neither UNWRA nor any other UN agency involved can offer more than palliative care while hostilities and confrontations drag on.[62]

On July 9, 2004, the ICJ ruled that that the 719-kilometre wall Israel was building to deter suicide bombers violated the human rights of Palestinians, as well as international law, and must be demolished where it passed through occupied territories, with payment of compensation. But only the Security Council could order demolition, something the US would surely veto, as it did when the Security Council sought to condemn the extra judicial killing of Hamas' spiritual leader in April 2004.

Refugee "host countries"—CASWANAME

UNHCR coined the acronym CASWANAME—the arc from Central Asia through Southwest Asia and the Middle East to North Africa—to describe its most concentrated area of activity, holding about 40% of all refugees under its wing. In recent years, Pakistan and Iran have had the most refugees at around one million each, principally from Afghanistan, but the outflow from Iraq through 2007 has boosted Syria and Jordan to near the same levels. Statistics are very fuzzy, given the difficulty of access for outsiders and in particular the number of Afghanis who may not be registered by anyone. Elsewhere, Germany and Tanzania in 2006 each had upwards of one-half million refugees of concern to UNHCR.

The US is credited with about 800,000 refugees and asylum seekers as of late 2006. (A methodology change doubled the number used in previous reports after UNHCR concluded that it should count the cumulative total inflow over 10 years, not five, as the average time required for arrivals to gain citizenship.) America remains, as cynics might say, the country everyone hates but to which everyone wants to migrate. Under the continued pressures of people on the move, an anti-immigrant mood applying to new foreigners of all categories has been building in the US as well as in Europe and Australia. In the US, the 9/11 attacks added a new dimension of concern, and some 1,000 aliens, including applicants for refugee status, were quickly rounded up to be detained without charge in violation of the Refugees Convention, exemplifying the dilution of rights that some governments have tried in the name of the "war on terror." Americans and Australians were officially urged to become more suspicious of strangers of any description, and "security" legislation was passed that undermined civil liberties in both countries.

Tensions continue to run high in many developed countries over refugee and immigrant admissions. The high percentage of those knocking on the door who are not "people like us" has fueled bias against Muslims in Europe and Hispanics in the US. There are voices for greater compassion in all the countries concerned, but no "durable solution" is in sight for many of the unfortunate populations who find themselves dispossessed of homes in 2007. And the US faces an enormous moral problem of what to do about the consequence of its 2003 invasion—Iraqi displaced persons and refugees, of whom it has taken but a handful.

Indigenous people—righting the wrongs of history

There is still controversy over how to define "indigenous people," but underlying any description, there is a long history of mistreatment. Typically, more powerful late-comers took their land by force, suppressed or destroyed their culture and traditional life-style, often repressed or eliminated their language, and in many cases compelled assimilation.

The ILO was the first modern international organization to try to provide some protection for the rights of indigenous people. Its first Convention on the subject was adopted in 1957, followed in 1989 by the Convention concerning Indigenous and Tribal Peoples in Independent Countries (No. 169). This Convention has secured only 17 ratifications, principally from European and Latin American countries. Its criteria for indigenous status include descent from people who occupied a country or region before conquest or colonization, and it provides for retention of those people's customs and institutions. Indigenous people, it also stated, had the right to choose their own development priorities, with prior and informed consent. The ILO Convention is the only treaty on the subject, and its application is limited.

In the 1980s, however, international concern started to gain momentum. In 1982 the World Bank issued a policy on indigenous peoples, the first international development body to do so. This was followed by a revised Operational Directive in 1991, urging full respect for indigenous peoples' dignity, human rights, and uniqueness, and the avoidance of damage to them by development activities. After public consultations with indigenous organizations, the Bank emphasized land rights and self determination more strongly in subsequent documents.

Declarations of Rights—re-righting history

The UN declared 1993 the Year for Indigenous Peoples and produced a draft declaration on their rights. It dealt with such issues as self determination, recognition of collective rights, prior informed consent, respect for indigenous culture and intellectual property, and recognition of indigenous people's institutions. It also sought to even up progress around the world, and called for restitution of land and resources, or for compensation. As an outcome of this work and of the Decade for Indigenous Peoples which followed (1994–2004), a new UN body, the Permanent Forum on Indigenous Issues, met for the first time in May 2002 in New York. More than six hundred indigenous people took part in what then became an annual consultation, reporting to ECOSOC on developmental, environmental, and human rights issues affecting indigenous people. Half of its 16 members are appointed by ECOSOC's president, and half nominated by governments and elected by ECOSOC, to serve three years and meet for ten days each year.

A final Declaration on the Rights of Indigenous Peoples was adopted by the General Assembly on September 13, 2007, in spite of resistance from the US, Australia, New Zealand, and Canada, the only four to vote against. They oppose what will likely be an ongoing forum for continuing criticism of their treatment of indigenous peoples and a channel to the UN for direct complaints. More to the point, perhaps, are concerns over indigenous challenges to national sovereignty, potential claims for billions in compensation and possible loss of access to indigenous land that contains, or may contain, large deposits of mineral and energy resources.

The four wealthy countries—the US, Australia, New Zealand and Canada—all have programs intended to help their sizeable and increasingly aware indigenous populations. With varying results, these governments have sought to assist political and social advancement while providing economic subsidies, but deplorable inequalities persist. America relies heavily on granting gambling rights, an approach which has assisted a smallish portion of its native population, made a number of outside investors obscenely wealthy, and done great collateral damage by fostering gambling addiction and crime.

Debate continues in all four countries on how better to address the problems of poverty, discrimination, crime violence and third world living standards that afflict many of their indigenous people (and not a few of their other citizens as well). The governments might benefit from working more closely with the UN system to bridge the gap of mistrust which can drive native populations to petition for the compassionate attention they don't see at home. But the issues have so many domestic political and economic stakeholders that it is virtually certain the governments will continue on present tracks, rejecting any significant engagement with UN machinery.

Many indigenous populations have fared badly in less wealthy countries where corruption and the greed of others make them and their land vulnerable to unchecked exploitation for commercial profit. Studies have found that indigenous peoples suffer higher rates of poverty, landlessness, malnutrition and internal displacement, and have lower levels of literacy and access to health care, compared to others in their countries of residence.[63] They have been given no special attention in the MDG process or in the Poverty Reduction Strategy

Papers produced by the regular development consultation process between governments, the IMF and the World Bank.

Implications for the UN and the US

The UN, with backing especially from NGOs, is the default conscience of the world for refugees, displaced persons and indigenous peoples. But the UN agencies can't do their work unless the member states provide material resources, and assure both access and security. As always, they are under strain to do so.

As the first decade of the millennium heads for its close, the world will be hard pressed to hold the line. Capacity—in both physical and emotional senses—to help is stretched by the numbers of those that are already in desperate need and those that seem to keep on coming. Resolution of long-term problems, notably those of the Palestinians, looks no nearer than before. The principal donor nations will still find substantial sums to fund assistance programs, but their concerns from social and economic pressures at home will limit the possibilities for resettlement and stiffen their resistance to "illegal" migration.

As with human rights, American NGOs have been in the front ranks of those seeking ways and means to help these unfortunate populations. Official Washington has been off on its own tracks—it will continue to write checks to help refugees and IDPs, but political realities and the press of issues associated with Iraq will preclude its taking any larger leadership role.

PART IV

To Promote Social Progress and Better Standards of Life

11

Reversing Poverty—Theories and Realities

"The mother of revolution and crime is poverty."

—Aristotle (384–322 B.C.)

The Preamble of the UN Charter expresses determination "to employ international machinery for the promotion of the economic and social advancement of all peoples." By sharing the world's wealth more widely, the drafters of the Charter sought to remove the motivation for war. This was not a new idea—people of all faiths have urged giving to the poor for centuries and hoped this would bring peace.

Undeniably, the UN and its agencies have helped the poor of the world through programs that have improved food production and water supplies, delivered emergency aid and food to populations in need, eradicated smallpox and reduced the spread of other diseases.[64] But development aid hasn't worked all that well, and the poor are still with us—of the world's 6.6 billion people, nearly one billion live on $1 or less a day.

To give better coherence to world development programs, the UN, with the encouragement of member governments, is focusing on eight broad Millennium Development Goals (MDGs). In this chapter, we consider the UN framework for development assistance and the first of the Goals, which is to reduce poverty. In the next chapter we look at the Goals aimed to improve health, provide essential education, and sustain the environment, and in Chapter 13 the final Goal—establishing a meaningful partnership for development between donors and we pull these parts together to assess the UN's responses to development in its broadest sense.

Development aid—the UN framework

The UN's founders set up a system with two primary pillars for promoting social progress and raising living standards: the Economic and Social Council (ECOSOC) was endowed with overall responsibility, and the Bretton Woods Institutions (the World Bank and the International Monetary Fund) were to supply the funds and build secure economies. The UN also drew into its global economic consultative network pre-existing bodies, including the World Health Organization, the International Labor Organization, and a host of other entities devoted to regulating and coordinating international activities. Many other bodies were soon also formed under the UN's aegis—UNICEF, UNDP, FAO, and WFP, to mention a few—and these were in turn joined by NGOs, of which some 1,500 now have consultative status with ECOSOC.

The Charter spelled out high goals for ECOSOC, but unlike the Security Council, gave it no authority over member states. ECOSOC can undertake studies and prepare reports, make recommendation and draft conventions for the UNGA, hold any number of international conferences, and furnish information to the Security Council—in short, facilitate others. In theory, it is empowered to coordinate the activities of the Specialized Agencies, but in practice they have paid attention to ECOSOC only when it suited them.

ECOSOC was originally given a manageable 18 members, but as UN membership grew, that was increased in 1965 to 27 and in 1973 to an unwieldy 54. Many of the added members, of course, were newly independent countries, which still find common cause in grievances against the industrialized world. These developing countries have occasionally put to good use ECOSOC's power to convene major conferences, and they continue to value the pulpit ECOSOC gives them, in part as "their" forum to offset the domination by wealthy governments of the World Bank and the IMF.

Territorial conflict was inevitable between ECOSOC on the one hand, and the World Bank and the International Monetary Fund on the other. Both sides have responsibility for addressing poverty and underdevelopment, but the Bank and the Fund have the money, and the Fund, moreover, has the power to make and enforce the rules. From the outset, the Bank and the Fund rejected coordination with ECOSOC and UN involvement with their budgets, while reserving the right to dictate economic orthodoxy to both the UN and developing countries.

Circling around the UN and its agencies in the economic and social firmament is a galaxy of NGOs. At their best, they support the UN by acting as a communications channel between the field and the center, supplying early warnings, collecting data, delivering assistance reliably, and monitoring the results. At their worst, according to their critics, NGOs are unaccountable, naive, political and the "soft arm of Western intervention."[65] But, whatever their faults, NGOs deliver help at the grass roots level and carry ever more of the burden to advocate for the poor and the oppressed.

In recent years, mega-philanthropy has also flowed into the breaches along with the resources of NGOs. Americans Bill Gates, Warren Buffett, Ted Turner and George Soros have allocated billions to support development projects. They and others have set up foundations, joining older established institutions like the venerable Ford Foundation, to provide seed money and grants, fund studies and consider innovative approaches to all facets of development assistance. But they have no magic bullets either.

Aid—theories and false starts

Aid as a serious multilateral concern began with the Bretton Woods agreement in 1944 that established the World Bank and the IMF. The Bank's first loan was to France for post-war reconstruction. The Bank moved its attention to newly independent developing countries, and aid orthodoxy for some years favored loans to them for large infrastructure projects—electric power plants, railways, and dams. The benefits of these big investments in fixed capital assets were optimistically expected to 'trickle down,' but many waited in vain for improved social services and land reform.

Other less than successful attempts followed. "Integrated rural development" embraced not only power and water, but also roads, bridges, ports, and irrigation. But bad projects, corruption and crushing debt service caused enormous problems, and when governments defaulted on their loans—as many did after the oil shocks of the 1970s—the Fund abandoned state regulation in favor of "structural adjustment" loans. The harsh conditions imposed by the Fund led to riots and in some poor countries to "unmitigated social and economic disaster."[66] Getting little credit for what *had* worked, the Bank and the Fund were reviled for what hadn't, including numerous projects that dislocated whole communities, destroyed forests or grasslands, and enriched the already rich. But those who permitted this and profited from it were mostly host country nationals, who were happy to scapegoat the Bank for national government shortcomings.

The Bank and the Fund, followed by many governments and by some NGOs, for a time tried meeting "basic human needs" or helping "the poorest of the poor." But such "back to basics" programs proved a disappointment in countries where needs far outstripped the capacity of external assistance, and where some governments were less interested in the plight of the poor than in controlling growing urban populations that might become restive. On their 50th anniversary in 1994/5, the Bank and the Fund found themselves besieged by jeering complaints from NGOs and aid recipients—mistrust lingers in many quarters.

The Bank's efforts were, of course, not all disasters. The "graduation" of developing countries to developed ones, particularly in East Asia, has been due in part to improvements in their economies that the Bank, the Asian Development Bank, and UN agencies made possible. Their success as exporters seemed to many to prove that trade is better than aid, and that a country that can fund most of its own development always does better than one that depends on outside institutions to do so. The Bank in its major 1998 study concluded that the accomplishment of "Asian tigers," China and India in contrast to much of Africa and parts of Latin America was due to sound government economic policy firmly implemented, but the definition and role of the policies concerned have been loudly questioned. Before assessing the debate still raging in 2007, it will be useful to consider the critical question of population growth.

Population growth—rights and choices

Too many people competing for scarce resources or too many children in a family unable to care for them can offset development gains. The relationship of population growth to economic development, however, is not a simple one, and researchers have found that much depends on circumstance and timing—it may be good, for example, to have young people coming into a growing economy, but there may later be a high price to pay if the same economy cannot sustain jobs over their life time. What is not disputable is that demographic change is a critical factor for both national planners and individual mothers.

The United Nations Population Fund (UNFPA, from its former name: the UN Fund for Population Activities) is the world's largest international source of funding for population and reproductive health programs. Since 1969, UNFPA has provided some $6 billion in assistance to developing countries. Over that time, access to voluntary family planning programs in developing countries has increased and fertility has fallen by half, from six children per woman to three. By 2004, nearly 60% of married women in developing countries had chosen to practice contraception, compared with 10–15% in 1969.

China became the first nation to restrict families to one child, not perfectly or humanely, but to considerable effect. In India under Indira Gandhi, forcible sterilization and inducements for contraception were tried but abandoned in the face of popular opposition, and Indian governments since then have been very cautious on the subject. Religious factions there and in many countries, including some democracies, seemingly try to out-populate their rivals, and the practice of polygamy remains widespread, particularly in Muslim countries. In the developed West, fertility levels are becoming unbalanced, and demographers anticipate that in a few decades there will be an old "European" and young Muslim population in Europe, and an old "American" and young Hispanic population in the United States.

The world's population of 7 billion is currently growing at 90 million a year, and the curve is not expected to flatten until the end of the 21st century, when there could be 11 billion people. The UN's population division in late 2003 projected a longer-term fall in global fertility leading to equilibrium at 9 billion in about three centuries. Based on 'medium-level' expectations that people in developing countries will come to want smaller families—which is by no means certain—the report predicted fertility rates will decline to two children per woman, and the average life expectancy will rise to more than 95 years by 2300, with average Japanese living more than 106. The exceptions to the trend were, of course, the 53 countries worst affected by HIV/AIDS, where rates of transmission and death were not expected to decline until at least 2010.

Predictions of a Malthusian doomsday are now rare, and much of the literature gives a sense that the projected increase in population can be "managed" with good development policies and sound social programs. Even under the best of circumstances, however, there will be setbacks of the kind reported recently by the UN Department of Economic and Social Affairs: "Because of population growth, the number of malnourished children in sub-Saharan Africa has actually increased from 29 million to 37 million over the period 1990 to 2003."[67]

The bottom line—does aid work?

Three seminal and scholarly books have recently presented expert arguments on aid and development—one professor is for more and rapid intervention by wealthy states, one against and one selects a bit of both approaches.

> **For aid**: The oracle of the UN's Millennium Development Goals, Columbia University's Jeffrey D. Sachs, says "We have the opportunity to end extreme poverty in our time." His book, *The End of Poverty: Economic Possibilities for Our Time*, published at the very end of 2006, lays out a plan to do it. The threshold he has in mind is lifting the poorest of the world above the $1 per day income on which nearly a billion people now subsist. To do so, he would apply more foreign aid from wealthy countries, including 0.7% of GNP from America which now gives a penurious 0.16%. By his analysis, the job can be done through programs to improve health, agricultural yields and transportation connectivity. Sachs has no doubt it is possible, and he presents a number of case studies and cogent arguments to prove his point.

> **Against aid:** Across town from Sachs, New York University's William Easterly draws almost the opposite conclusion in *The White Man's Burden: Why the West's Efforts to Aid the Rest Have Done So Much Ill and So Little Good*, also published in 2006. Easterly delivers a scathing attack on Sachs, the UN, the World Bank and anyone else who might presume to prescribe development for poor country patients. He rejects global assistance plans—by extension of this argument, he does not offer one of his own—and praises in contrast initiatives and incentives that spring from each distinctive country situation. With fervor equal to that of Sachs, he too presents case studies and cogent arguments to prove his points.

> **For and against aid:** From across the Atlantic, Oxford's Paul Collier gives a different perspective in his 2007 work, *The Bottom Billion: Why the Poorest Countries are Failing and What Can be Done About It*. Collier sees the least developed nations caught in one or more of four traps: bad governance, civil conflict, being landlocked, and possessing natural resources in circumstances that encourage grossly disruptive exploitation, as for example, by gangs expropriating diamonds or drugs. Like Easterly, he is scornful of misguided foreign aid, but like Sachs, he sees foreign aid as a critical part of the solution

when properly applied. His own mix of instruments comprises aid, trade policy, military intervention where needed to buy time for development to take hold, and a set of international "charters" that would use laws in the West to track monetary deposits of corrupt rulers, regulate trade in natural resources, and promote media freedom. Collier's beliefs are also passionately held and based on scholarly research.

All three professors are surely right up to a point, and all provide valuable new insights into how compassionate programs of the North should help the poorest of the South. It is tempting for the layperson to side with Collier as the reasonable compromise, and his views have gained considerable attention, but it does not look like his menu of "instruments" can or will be adopted wholesale anytime soon by governments, international organizations or NGOs.

There have been some innovative breakthroughs. The brightest example is perhaps the Nobel Peace Prize-winning work of Muhammad Yunus and his Grameen Bank, that since 1976 has made small loans to poor people, many of them women, in Bangladesh. Microloans have become so fashionable that high school students in rich countries have established funds for African village women. A more recent example of progress from "outside-the-box" thinking is the very successful "conditional cash transfer" programs adopted by Brazil, Mexico and other Latin American governments, which give cash to poor families for sending kids to schools or utilizing health services. As valuable as they are, however, microloans and cash transfers are not panaceas.

A sober 2007 review by the World Bank's chief economist and an IMF colleague found that "evidence on aid effectiveness is fragile"—meaning it has yet to be shown unambiguously that aid results in economic development. But as their report goes on to say, that does not mean "all aid is ineffective, nor that little is known about how to make aid more effective." The problem as they see it is how to complete the chain from donors to policy makers to policies to outcomes.[68] "Elementary, my dear Watson," as Holmes might say, but anyone experienced in development issues will recognize the familiar difficulty of getting governments in developing countries to use aid effectively for the benefit of the intended recipients.

Trade, not aid—but politics rules

"Trade, not aid" is a slogan that has been bruited about since the 1980s. According to Oxfam, poor countries make 32 times as much from exports, even at their current levels, than they receive from aid. An increase of as little as one percent in each developing region's share of world exports would reduce the number of the world's extremely poor by 128 million, or 12%.[69] UN agencies like UNDP and FAO regularly stress the obvious value of greater market access for developing country products.

But governments of the North still impose conditionality on aid and protect politically sensitive trade sectors. The EU has for decades subsidized its beet sugar at the expense of the developing world's far cheaper, unsubsidized cane sugar. The Europeans also allow raw coffee and chocolate to enter free of duty, but prevent the producer countries from processing it, so the value of the product becomes disproportionately higher than the raw material. In the 1990s when the US subsidized 25,000 cotton farmers to the tune of $3.9 billion, three times its aid budget for Africa, world prices fell by 26%, sabotaging the incomes of millions of farmers in poor countries. Significantly, the US was eventually found to be in breach of WTO rules, showing that the multilateral system can work, although many US agricultural subsidies continue, and Congress ties food aid to American producers and shippers. China also ties its aid programs, and buys raw materials in African countries for finished manufactures, which are sometimes sold back to the detriment of fledgling local industries.

Negotiations on the "Doha round" of talks to improve the world trade system have hung up on the unwillingness, primarily on the part of the Europeans to cut agricultural supports. The US claims to be ready to reduce its subsidies, but only if the Europeans do. (A 2005 UN General Assembly resolution calling for progress in the Doha round to enhance market access carried by 121 votes for, 51 abstentions and a single vote against from the US.) The Cairns Group of agricultural exporting countries can count some successes in penetrating protected markets, and it generally supports the developing countries, led by India, Brazil, China and South Africa, which are pressing the issue in talks with the US and EU, unsuccessfully so as of mid-2007.

The Millennium Development Goals—order out of chaos?

Looking to the UN's 2000 Millennium Summit, Secretary General Annan pulled together the experience of UN agencies and donor countries to set forth specific development goals, expanding on proposals made by OECD in 1996. World leaders in their 2005 Summit Declaration approved a series of pledges to tackle poverty, help the vulnerable, protect the environment and more. Finally, the UN Secretariat distilled the Declaration's language down to eight Millennium Development Goals (MDGs) for bettering the welfare of the world's poor by 2015.

The eight Goals aim to 1) eradicate extreme poverty and hunger, 2) achieve universal primary education, 3) promote gender equality and empower women, 4) reduce child mortality, 5) improve maternal health, 6) combat HIV/AIDS, malaria, and other diseases, 7) ensure environmental sustainability and 8) build a global partnership for development. As we shall see, there has been important progress, but half way into the 15 year period, the record of performance is mixed, a number of goals will not be achieved if present trends continue, and sub-Saharan Africa lags the rest of the world.

MDG 1 is of particular relevance to the issue we have taken up here: aid programs to promote development and reduce poverty. We will address the other MDGs in succeeding chapters.

MDG 1—eradicate extreme poverty and hunger

MDG 1 sets two prime goals: to halve the proportion of people living on less than a dollar a day, and to halve the number of those who suffer from hunger (the target year is 2015 to be measured against the situation in 1990). The target populations are the almost one billion people living on less than a dollar a day, the 800 million who are malnourished, and the 153 million children under five who are underweight. The World Bank has the lead for the poverty reduction target, UNICEF and FAO for attacking hunger. There is something to build on since the number of people living on less than $1 per day has reduced by nearly one third since the 1980s, thanks mainly to gains in East Asia.

The UN predicted in 2007 that the targets could be met for the world as a whole and for most, but not all, of its regions.[70] In sub-Saharan Africa, the poverty rate had declined by 6% since 2000, but the poverty reduction target for MDG 1 will not be met there or in parts of Southern Asia. Similarly for hungry children, the UN's midpoint review concluded, "If current trends continue, the target of halving the proportion of underweight children will be missed by 30 million children, largely because of slow progress in Southern Asia and sub-Saharan Africa."

The UN's statistical analysis of progress towards MDG 1 at the 2005 mid-point shows there have been success and failures in individual countries in all developing regions. Some factors of course have been beyond the control of the UN and the aid donor community—the economic wrench that followed the collapse of the Soviet Union in Central Asia, and conflict in sub-Saharan Africa and instability in West Asia. And natural disasters, including drought and the ravages of AIDS,' have sapped the strength and resources of all concerned.

The UN report's finding for Asia and the Pacific region, which has the largest number of poor, is that three elements are necessary. First, growth has to be targeted to benefit the poor through building their capacity and providing social protections systems for the disadvantaged. Second, external assistance is required, especially for least-developed and landlocked or small island states, to build physical infrastructure and institutions. Finally, there is a need to improve governance, reduce corruption and deliver social services to the poor. To deal with hunger in places like sub-Saharan Africa, the report concluded there must be more investment in agriculture, including research and education, and in physical infrastructure—two major sectors which have suffered from recent declines in public investment and external development assistance.

Donor governments, the US among them, know the MDG 1 target to reduce the proportion of malnourished children is falling short, but so far none have stepped forward to boost the effort. Competition for resources is stiff, and as of 2007, there are no obvious major shifts or quantum increases in the works to provide the needed increments. It is sobering in any case to reflect that even if MDG 1 goals were to be fully met, as of 2015 there would still be hundreds of millions of people around the globe subsisting on less than $1 per day and tens of millions of malnourished children under five.

12

Health, Education, and the Environment—Getting Better?

o o o o o o o o o o o o o o o o o o o o o o o o o o o o o o o o o o o

"Are we on course to look back, in 2015, and say that no effort was spared?"

—*Kofi Annan, Annual Report of the Secretary-General, 2006*

As with so much the UN seeks to do, eliminating poverty means dealing with many interconnected factors—health, education, water and sanitation to name only four.[71] Thus, of the eight Millennium Development Goals, three focus directly on health, two on education and one on sustaining the environment.

Many of us are conditioned to think that raising incomes of the poor is the way to solve development problems. That approach hasn't worked very well, least of all for those countries still caught in cruel poverty traps that have defied solution and left millions sick, unschooled, and without clean water. Nobelist Amartya Sen's research has shown that sensible policies can bring about better health and education even if low incomes persist. The MDGs are pointed in that direction.

2007 may go down as the year the planet woke up to the threat of global warming. The UN's Intergovernmental Panel on Climate Change and Al Gore shared the Nobel Peace Prize for demonstrating the urgency and scope of pending disasters from global warming. The poor need clean water and sanitation—the rest of the world, which takes such things for granted, needs for its part to face up to the far broader implications of its wasteful ways. Mass migrations and wars over water loom on the horizon, not as the stuff of science fiction, but as possible news headlines later in this century.

The problems of meeting basic human needs and sustaining the environment are interlocked and potentially self-perpetuating. Experts and politicians continue to argue over relative priorities and what works best where. The following sections recap the main features of the global effort—where does it stand and what are its prospects?

Health—the "first wealth"

The UN, through WHO, UNICEF and other agencies, has won high praise for combating diseases, notably for eradication of smallpox, control of polio and tetanus, mitigation of HIV/AIDS and measures to contain threats like SARS and the Ebola virus. WHO set itself the smallpox task in 1967 and achieved its goal ten years later at a cost of some $300 million. Another success, less well known, is the Iodine Deficiency Disorders (IDD) program that, using simple interventions in countries where leached soils produce deficiency diseases, has reversed rates of cretinism and goiter. Iodine deficiency is recognized as the world's most preventable cause of brain damage, and by 2000 almost 70% of households had access to iodized oil or salt that, taken before pregnancy, kept almost 80 million babies from being born with the deficiency.

Threats to health, of course, can and do readily cross national boundaries if initial outbreaks are not contained at once. Cases in recent years of 'mad cow' disease, bird flu, SARS, horse flu, Ebola and dengue fever have shown how careless practices in a few places can quickly endanger human life in many others. Plant and animal diseases and pests are as mobile as modern humans, and UN agencies are in the front line of defense.

Combating a particular disease can be done systematically, but assuring health is a far more complex challenge. For example, the fourth of the MDGs commits UN member states to reducing by two thirds the mortality of children under five by 2015. While many die from childhood diseases that are easily treated or prevented by immunization, in poverty-stricken areas health is always undermined by combinations of problems. Many children lack access to sanitation, and an estimated 153 million are underweight because they have inadequate food, intestinal parasites, or insufficient care. Those in tropical climates get malaria. In places where electricity is unavailable or unreliable, the very fact that vaccines cannot be refrigerated inhibits progress with immunization.

Maternal mortality, a central target of MDG 5, is a similarly complex undertaking when it comes to finding a long-term, comprehensive solution. Sub-standard care underpins the deplorable numbers in the poorest countries, but more than that, pregnant women and mothers with infants often get caught up in crushing webs of conflict, poverty, illiteracy, and gender discrimination. This dismaying picture along with lagging aid inputs means the target of a 75% reduction over the maternal mortality ratios of 1990 is not expected to be met in Africa, most of Asia (except East Asia), Latin America or Oceania.

Malaria and tuberculosis—new hope

The MDGs focused new attention on tuberculosis (TB) and malaria, which remain among the leading causes of death world-wide and strike poor people the hardest. A UN report in January 2005 noted that malaria kills as many people *every month* as the 2004 Indian Ocean tsunami did. In Africa, the disease kills one million people a year, and it causes as many as 90% of deaths of children under five. Remarkable results have been achieved with targeted programs using insecticide treated nets and related measures—in Kenya for example, with a grant from the Global Fund to Fight AIDS, TB and Malaria, authorities distributed 3.4 million such nets and deaths of children from malaria dropped 44% in the area covered.[72]

TB causes more deaths than malaria and is especially lethal in combination with HIV. Evolution of new drug-resistant TB strains has added to the problem. WHO launched a new Stop TB Strategy in 2006 with a strong focus on detection as well as treatment. Statistics indicate the global incidence of TB may have peaked in 2005—the WHO and MDG targets for cutting prevalence and death rates should be met by 2015 in all WHO regions except Eastern Europe and Africa.[73]

By 2007, the UN's report on progress towards the MDGs showed a decline in childhood deaths from preventable diseases everywhere but sub-Saharan Africa and South Asia. WHO reports[74] that measles is still a leading killer of young children, even though a safe and effective vaccine has been available for over 40 years—over 95% of deaths occur in poorer countries because of failure to vaccinate infants. Deaths from measles dropped by 60% as of 2005 compared to 2000 as a result of vigorous international efforts spurred by the 2001 Measles Initiative in Africa (with extensive US public and private participation) and World Health

Assembly decisions in 2003 and 2005. A wide variety of NGOS and govern-ments have joined with WHO and UNICEF to expand the Measles Initiative and campaign for a 90% (or greater) vaccination rate and stronger surveillance.

UN agencies like UNICEF do much of the delivery work, but the leading donor in child health is now the Gates Foundation. Bill and Melinda Gates have pledged $750 million to help vaccinate children in poor countries, and called for world leaders to help find the additional $12 billion dollars needed to protect 10 million children from communicable diseases. But most governments still shy away from major increases in aid programs.

HIV/AIDS—outpacing the response

Since their discovery in Africa in 1981, the Human Immunodeficiency Virus (HIV) and Acquired Immunodeficiency Syndrome (AIDS) have spread rapidly to every country in the world, with 39.5 million cases of people living with AIDS reported at the end of 2006 Of those, the largest proportion were in sub-Saharan Africa. In 2006, 4.3 people were newly infected with HIV, with the fastest rates of infection occurring in East Asia and the Commonwealth of Independent States.

The number of deaths from AIDS also increased, from 2.2 million a year in 2001 to 2.9 million in 2006. The daily death rate from AIDS is reported to be 1,300, or 3 million a year. More than 20 million people have died since the disease was first diagnosed. Infection caused from tainted injection needles was on the rise in Africa, while in parts of Asia the main cause of new infections was unprotected sex with sex workers and between men.[75]

UNAIDS, the body that coordinates the world effort, summed up the problem in a September 2007 report. The AIDS epidemic, it said, has shortened life expect-ancy in many countries by more than 20 years and despite global progress in expanding access to antiretroviral therapy, more than 70% of people in need did not have access to treatment in 2006. The report noted that AIDS funding had increased exponentially from $300 million in 1996 to around $10 billion for 2007, but sums on the order of $40 to 60 billion would be necessary to provide universal access to care by 2015.

Dr Peter Piot, UNAIDS Executive Director, said in his 2004 biannual report that the AIDS epidemic continued to outpace the global response, and that no region in the world was spared. In poor countries, only 10% of HIV infected people were getting treatment. Among the cultural difficulties facing UNAIDS are the denial of responsibility by many in poor countries, reluctance to educate people about the causes of AIDS, prevalence of inaccurate beliefs about the disease, and refusal to practice safe sex or safe drug injection.

MDG 6 sets as a target halting the increase of HIV/AIDS by 2015 and beginning to reverse its spread. A major challenge is to deliver treatment to the poor at costs they can afford. Despite the many expressions of official concern and intensified efforts, this target is not expected to be achieved anywhere, and sub-Saharan Africa will remain the worst affected.

Education—millions still left behind

The drafters of the Universal Declaration of Human Rights called education an "empowerment right," one upon which other rights—civil, political, economic, and social—depend. One of the UN's first agencies, the UN Educational, Scientific, and Cultural Organization (UNESCO) was set up in 1945. Member states are obliged under subsequent Human Rights Covenants to pursue the goal of providing education of good quality to all their people.

UNESCO was authorized to operate across five thematic areas: education, natural sciences, social and human sciences, communications and information, and culture. Among other activities, it undertook cultural preservation, protected intellectual property and world heritage, and fostered the independence of news media. It was over press freedom that the US left UNESCO in 1984 at the height of the Third World's New International Information Order campaign, which decried imbalances from developed country control of world media. By 1997, UNESCO had been brought back to the center, and in 2003, the US rejoined, saying the organization had made financial and management reforms, and revived its founding principles, especially press freedom.

UNESCO plays a coordinating role for education programs across the UN system, while UNICEF and UNDP have had the operational lead, partnering with a variety of organizations, including the World Bank, to expand schooling. Gains across the board have been impressive over the last decade, but statistics don't always give the full picture. UNICEF reported in May 2007, for example, that although official school records showed 77 million children not enrolled in primary school, household surveys indicated a total closer to 104 million. The same report also pointed up that quality of education has not kept pace with expanded enrollment. UNICEF hopes to harness the new interagency "cluster approach" to address these problems and improve outcomes.

MDG 2—primary education for all children by 2015—is within reach. The UN's 2007 MDG Report recorded major increases since 1999 to the point where world-wide 88% of children were enrolled in primary school. That still left 72 million out, and, not surprisingly, girls and children from poorer and rural families were the most likely to be left behind. The biggest problem area, also no surprise, is sub-Saharan Africa, where enrollment had reached only 70%—an extra push, which had not materialized by 2007, will be needed if the target is to be attained there.

MDG 3 tackles gender disparity, and for schooling, it proposes to equalize participation in primary and secondary education by 2015. The UN's 2007 MDG Progress Chart shows girls already at or close to parity and expected to reach the target in all regions except sub-Saharan Africa. Even there, the 2007 assessment is "almost close to parity." (The second MDG 3 goal of increasing women's share of paid employment is projected to fall short in all of Africa and Asia, except for East Asia.)

The environment—the heat is on

The series of highly authoritative scientific reports from the UN's Intergovernmental Panel on Climate Change (IPCC) and Al Gore's dramatic film, *An Inconvenient Truth*, in early 2007 quieted, but still did not silence, US environment skeptics led by the White House. President Bush has said he recognizes the seriousness of the problem, but he continues to advance a voluntary approach, despite calls from environmentalists and most western democracies for mandatory measures.

In 1987 the Brundtland Commission effectively changed the world's thinking from a confrontation between environment and development to a joint project: "sustainable development." Twenty years later, the heat is on: as a result of a six fold population increase, deforestation, and the burning of fossil fuels, the world is seven degrees (Celsius scale) hotter than it was in the industrial revolution. With 2 billion more humans expected in the world by 2030, the consequences of continued steady increase in energy consumption would be dire indeed. A common cause of the collapse of so many civilizations in history, Jared Diamond proposed in *Collapse* (2005), was the destruction of the environmental resources on which they depended.

Following on Brundtland's contribution, the UN Intergovernmental Panel on Climate Change (IPCC—the 2007 Nobel Peace Prize co-recipient) was set up in 1988. Open to all UN member states, the IPPC brings together the world's experts to periodically evaluate the latest information and research on climate change. In 2007, it delivered its Fourth Assessment, which made definitive findings on the dangerous pace of global warming and the responsibility of human activity for the change.

The UN Earth Summit in Rio de Janeiro put reduction of man-made greenhouse gas emissions on the world agenda in 1992. Participants at the Summit concluded the UN Framework Convention on Climate (UNFCC), obliging all signatory states, including the US, to voluntarily cut back on greenhouse gas emissions to reduce the rate of global warming. It had no mandatory provisions, no enforcement and no targets, but the text provided for additional agreements, called protocols, to address these possibilities.

Kyoto Protocol—what next?

The Kyoto Protocol of 1997 added to the Convention a limit for emissions by each industrialized country, but did not similarly restrict developing countries. The Protocol became a binding treaty for signatories on February 16, 2005, and 34 industrialized nations undertook to reduce their carbon dioxide emissions by 5.2% of 1990 levels by 2012. Some were allowed large increases in their emissions, while others agreed to large cuts, and a system of carbon trading was set up for sales of carbon credits to offset contributions to emissions.

The US, which is responsible for 36.1% of greenhouse gas emissions from the industrialized world, refused to ratify the Protocol, as did the Howard Government in Australia (emitting 2.1%), and a handful of smaller emitters. They complained that the reduction targets didn't apply to Brazil, China, and India, because they were classed as developing countries. They have a point since India and China particularly are industrializing at an extraordinary pace, increasing their energy consumption, and lobbying to sit at the world's top-level economic policy-making tables, but for the purposes of the Kyoto Protocol, India and China cry poor. Developing countries were expected to account for more than half of global emissions by 2020.

Global warming was at the top of the UNGA agenda for the annual New York gathering of world leaders in September 2007, and Secretary General Ban called a special convocation of leaders to address the subject. Bush snubbed the event and instead invited counterparts to meet with him in Washington where he urged a program of voluntary curbs, denounced by environmental advocates as totally inadequate to the purpose.

The first phase of the Kyoto Protocol measures will conclude in 2012. The Protocol itself will remain in force, and proponents of mandatory emission reductions are actively working for a follow-on program. The US, Australia, China and India have found common ground in emphasizing technology instead of mandatory emission targets, and in January 2006, the four were joined by Japan and South Korea to launch the Asia-Pacific Partnership on Clean Development and Climate to promote that approach.

Whatever kind of concerted international action comes next in 2012 depends in large part on domestic politics in the US, Australia and Canada. They are the only three major developed countries with governments that oppose the Kyoto approach, although polls in all three have indicated that public opinion favors supporting the Protocol. Other western democracies, especially those in the EU, continue to be strong advocates for mandatory targets to reduce emissions.

MDG 7—going for environmental basics

MDG 7 seeks to ensure environmental sustainability. It targets common problems of water, sanitation, poor human habitats, and loss of environmental resources. Heading off an acute water shortage is one of the world's most urgent tasks, and hence an high priority for the UN and the World Bank. Access to safe drinking water is part of this picture, and in urban areas around the world there has been a decline, although in rural areas, all global regions show some progress. Encouragingly, UNICEF and WHO found that by 2002, 83% of the world's people had water either in their homes or within a 30 minute walk—a rise from 1990 levels of 77%. The Goal for 2015 of 88.5% appears to be within reach, although once again sub-Saharan Africa lags behind.

MDG 7 also sets targets bettering the lot of the 2.6 billion people currently without access to adequate sanitation. This and safe water are twinned major problems for sub-Saharan Africa, Oceania and Central Asia, where at the current pace the MDG target will not be reached. More generally, the MDG goal of significantly improving the lives of at least 100 million slum dwellers by 2020 will also fall short in large swaths of Africa and Asia.

Another facet of MDG 7 is its intent to reverse deforestation, halt the loss of biodiversity and conserve energy supplies. New tree planting and conservation measures have improved the picture somewhat in recent years, but the threat to biodiversity, in particular old-growth forest ecosystems and fish stocks, remains serious in most areas of he globe. About 200 square kilometers of forest still disappear every day, and only 22% of world fisheries are now sustainable compared to 40% in 1975. Far more intense effort is needed if the declines are to be reversed by 2015 ... or anytime in this century.

13

Human Development—Aid, Globalization and Democracy

○ ○
Human development is first and foremost about allowing people to lead a life that they value and enabling them to realize their potential as human beings.

—Foreword, Human Development Report 2006, UNDP

The UN is where all the threads come together for the world's effort to promote prosperity and the pursuit of happiness, or as the UN Charter puts it, "better standards of life in larger freedom."

UN and donor government aid programs are of course only part of the picture. Globalization is adding new dimensions to the concept of interdependence—with good and bad consequences for developing countries. Democracy has been on the march, but doesn't always equate to good governance, which is perhaps the single most critical factor for sound development and good use of foreign assistance.

Can new forms of cooperation help harness globalization and improve governance to bridge the development gap? It would seem that everything has been tried at least once, but despite all the experience we have to draw on, there is no guarantee of progress.

We look next at the overarching issues facing the UN system and sum up the prospects for the long-sought more effective partnership between aid recipients, the UN system, donor countries, and NGOs.

Globalization—the good, the bad and the uncertain

Will globalization help or hinder the effort to make the world a more prosperous and equitable place? Those, especially in the developing world, who want to preserve cultural autonomy and promote a fairer distribution of wealth are leery of globalization, until it can be shown to deliver better opportunities, greater fairness, genuinely free trade, and cheaper medicines. They are also concerned that more rapid transfers of goods, services, information and capital may not extend to equally free movement of people from place to place, thus robbing the poor of equal opportunity.

In any case, globalization is a process that cannot be stopped, and it need not conflict with the purposes of the UN. As Secretary General, Kofi Annan sought to link globalization to Charter ideals through a new partnership of governments, civil society and business. The effort was made more difficult after American neo-cons rose to power in 2000 with a vision that largely dismissed the UN and multilateral institutions.

The UN's top leadership has continued to perceive globalization as a potential force for good. Annan proposed in 1999 and nurtured through to the end of his reign in 2006 a unique voluntary "framework" organization, called the Global Compact, that brings together UN officials, big company CEOs, labor leaders, and NGO chiefs to support UN goals. After replacing Annan, Ban Ki-moon continued the project and in July 2007, at a summit meeting in Switzerland, the Global Compact issued a "Geneva Declaration" with strong language on promoting sustainable markets, protecting the environment, fighting corruption and improving labor conditions.

But, as the history of the UN makes clear, such high-flown declarations lead only slowly, if at all, to meaningful action. Many activists remain to be convinced the Compact will in fact strong-arm governments or corporations to change their ways when substantial profits are at stake. The Compact's language is vague, it operates by invitation only and to some degree lacks the transparency associated with UN entities. 151 NGOs sent an open letter in October 2007 to the UN's man in charge of the Compact, Under Secretary John Ruggie, urging more forceful action with specific standards and mandatory provisions.

How well the Compact succeeds remains to be seen, but it is an imaginative effort to cross the divide between the forces now represented by the corporation-oriented World Economic Forum (WEF) on the one hand and the social-activist driven World Social Forum (WSF) on the other. For years, the WEF, better known simply as Davos after the Swiss town where it meets annually in January, has been the premier convocation of business and government leaders. It grew to attract some 100 CEOs of the world's 500 biggest companies along with top economic and financial officials from every country that counts. Its agenda progressively widened to include discussion of climate change, Islam, poverty, the US deficit, and HIV/AIDs.

The elitist character of the annual meeting in Davos inspired those excluded to create an "anti-Davos" for the increasing number of activists protesting the dark sides of globalization and transnational corporate activities. The WSF began in 2001, emphasizing respect for human rights, the environment, social justice, equality and "the sovereignty of peoples." In Nairobi, Kenya, the 2007 WSF had about 75,000 attendees, representing 1,400 organizations from 110 countries. Described by its supporters as a Carnival of the Oppressed, and by some observers as an NGO Fair, the 2007 WSF aimed among other things to promote a fairer, healthier, cleaner version of global trade and cancel what it called the "criminal debt" owed by many poor nations. The WSF has been criticized from within for being long on rhetoric and short on action, and for allowing NGOs to displace genuine popular movements in its representation.

Good governance—democracy is not enough

Good governance is a critical factor in any developing country's ability to deal with the pressures of globalization and benefit from the inputs of external assistance. The West tends to simplistically equate good governance with democracy, and there has been a concerted effort to bring democracies of varying stripe together to exert more potent economic as well as political influence on international affairs. Spearheaded by the US, a ministerial meeting in June 2000 issued the Warsaw Declaration, which asserted that peace, development, human rights, and democracy were interdependent, and laid the foundation for a formal Community of Democracies (CD). By 2005, the CD mustered some 160 representatives of member states and agencies for a meeting in Santiago. Although the CD has no permanent secretariat and its membership qualifications remain ill-defined, it has met as a "democracy caucus" at the UN since September 2004, and Mali was scheduled to host its next Ministerial Conference in November 2007.

A mere 54 countries were democracies in 1980, but by 2000, an estimated 121 countries had some or all of the elements of formal, if not necessarily liberal, democracy. In thirty years, the number of democracies in the world has almost trebled, and according to Freedom House in New York, 119 nations, or 62%, of the 192 UN members are now democratic. 'Democracy' is nowhere mentioned in the UN Charter, but especially since the end of the Cold War, the UN has propagated electoral democracy "as the basic governance template for all nations to follow."[76] More than half the total of UNDP program expenditure went into governance, particularly to support democratic transition processes, in 166 countries. In the decade to 2002, the UNDP helped prepare more than 270 reports that related governance and democracy to human development and poverty reduction.

The World Bank's 1998 report *Assessing Aid: What Works, What Doesn't, and Why* found that the key to reducing poverty is good policy produced by improved governance, based on democracy, transparency, and accountability. There is still disagreement over what exactly constitutes good policy for any given country, but enthusiasm for *good governance* displaced the belief in *small government* that prevailed in the 1980s. The change involved more than a generational buzzword—the popularity of governance in development thinking with its stress on citizen participation and sustainable human development overtook the previous emphasis on growth.

Good theory, but in developing nations pervasive and deep-rooted corruption time and again has sucked the life blood out of democratic government. Corrupt 'facilitation' payments occur in many countries and at all levels in society, but dictatorships and immature democracies have produced the highest achievers: Presidents Suharto (personal wealth $15 to 35 billion), Marcos ($5–10 billion), Mobutu ($5 billion), Abacha ($2–5 billion), Duvalier ($300–800 million), Fujimori ($600 million), and Estrada ($78–80 million).[77] Much, although by no means all, of this money was siphoned off from foreign aid programs run with the best of intentions by UN agencies, IFIs, governments and NGOs, who paid the high price of doing business with such governments in hopes of reaching past them to the desperate people at the end of the delivery chain.

In the 1990s, the donor community, led by its premier club, the Organization for Economic Development and Cooperation (OECD), began to stress "development partnerships" with attention to improvements on both the donor and recipient sides. In May 1995, an OECD Development Assistance Committee observed, "More widespread and sustainable progress now depends on building strong capacities to achieve good governance, reduce poverty, and protect the environment." The same Committee a year later published *Shaping the 21st Century: the Contribution of Development Co-operation,"* which elaborated on the partnership concept and set forth a set of achievable goals, the precursor to the MDGs.

MDG 8. Develop a global partnership for development

Supporting all the first seven Goals, MDG 8 calls for a "partnership" with obligations on both donors and recipients of aid. The onus is on developed countries to free up access to their markets and technology, and to create an environment in which development can flourish—and most importantly, to pay for development of the poor countries. The requirement for developing countries is to create good governance and to focus on the social needs and human capital of their own people—and most importantly, not to pocket the aid money.

In 2002, the UN organized a Global Conference on Financing for Development in Monterrey, Mexico. Participants claimed a "Monterrey Consensus" had been reached on mobilizing additional resources for assistance and making structural changes in developing countries, but the terms were vague and commitments uncertain. President Bush announced a $5 billion increase (50%) in ODA, but the US, the world's largest donor of ODA in cash terms and a significant donor of private aid, remains one of the stingiest official donors in proportion to GDP (0.16%), and like the Europeans, has been a significant subsidizer and protector of its own agriculture.

The ODA increase promised by Bush at Monterrey is to be distributed by the Millennium Challenge Corporation, a US semi-private body created for the purpose of assuring that aid goes only to governments that meet standards for good economic policy, including low corruption. The idea is an old one and the principle is incorporated as indicated above in MDG 8, but the US program has more explicit links to recipient country performance. One major problem of course is that the US approach offers no hope for help to many of the most needy, namely the poor people living under incompetent governments that can't or won't meet the governance requirements.

In December 2006, Spain established a $700 million UN Fund for the Achievement of Millennium Development Goals. The fund will be jointly managed by the Government of Spain and the UNDP, with a steering committee including development experts to allocate grants for projects supporting the MDGs. Spain's joint effort with UNDP contrasts for better or worse with the US Millennium Challenge Account, set up to operate independently of the UN.

Official development assistance (ODA) and debt relief rose significantly in 2005, and in the same year major donors issued the Paris Declaration on Aid Effectiveness, which promised substantial improvements in the quality of aid from the donor side. The UN was able to report debt service payments had fallen as a proportion of export revenues of developing countries between 1990 and 2005. New money has flowed from "emerging" donors: China, Venezuela and Saudi Arabia are among governments that have increased the aid pot along with private sources such as the Gates Foundation. Also, a "Leading Group on Solidarity Levies to Fund Development," started at the initiative of the Brazilian and French presidents, has grown to 46 participants and begun to raise money for development aid through levies on airline tickets and currency transactions—Washington has adamantly opposed any such tax.

Still, the MDG 8 partnership remains elusive. The Bush Administration, leery of targets especially those related to donor aid levels, has maintained a certain distance and left the initiative to others. Disagreements persist over the level of financing for the MDGs, how far to go in untying aid and reducing agricultural subsidies, how much voice to give developing countries in IMF and World Bank Councils, and the acceptability of "solidarity levies." There has been little progress on these issues in preparatory discussions for the Second Global Conference on Financing Development, scheduled for 2008 in Doha (completely separate from the Doha round of trade talks). Since the US Presidential campaign will be in full swing in 2008, no breakthroughs are likely, and the next comprehensive assessment of MDG prospects will probably come only in 2009 or 2010 when the new Administration in Washington gets its feet on the ground.

14

Conclusion—The Right Policy for America

○ ○

"More than ever before in human history, we share a common destiny. We can master it only if we face it together. And that, my friends, is why we have the United Nations."

—*Kofi Annan, Message for the New Millennium,*
December 1999

The United Nations Headquarters building—the soaring glass-fronted tower in New York City—looks virtually the same as it did when it was built in 1950, a symbol of hope for people around the world. But years of wear and tear have taken their toll. The complex needs an overhaul to restore aging parts and build in modern operating systems. Fortunately, help is on the way. After much wrangling over cost and means, member states have agreed on a plan, and the initial contract has been signed.

Like its home office structure, the UN itself was designed in a previous era, has been buffeted by time and requires modernization. In contrast to the fate of the building, however, the rancorous debate of member states has yet to come to closure on how best to proceed. Clearly, the UN can do better, and it can do more—so could governments around the world. The tough questions for the UN are how to reconcile competing priorities of its membership, overcome the systemic defects of its large bureaucracies, and tackle security and human rights problems that fester outside its reach because of member state gridlock. Years of negotiation have brought some improvements, but the maladies linger on.

150

The frustration in capitals is evident. Many serious thinkers consider the UN "ineffective," especially when the world's most pressing security problems are up for action. Recent Secretaries General have pledged to work for restoration of trust in the organization, but recurrent scandals and spats with unhappy members have regularly thrown them off stride. Mr. Ban made no great breakthroughs during his initial months on the job.

Reform to the rescue?

Reform is everyone's deus ex machina to revitalize the UN. And why not? Governments and businesses around the world have well-developed techniques to bolster large organizations by identifying weaknesses and introducing best practices: accountability, transparency, professionalism, measurable results, benchmarks, cost-effectiveness, oversight, and so on. But at the UN perverse political infighting—the bugaboo of open and pluralistic entities everywhere—continues to intrude.

The competition for influence in the UN has stakeholders locked in sterile bureaucratic combat. The major agendas of competing groups can scarcely be called hidden, but neither are they stated forthrightly. Debates continue to be popularity contests more than constructive exchanges as all the parties hold their ground, pandering to domestic constituencies. The governments of the South present themselves as David against Goliath, those of the North as Galahad out to save oppressed people from their own governments, and Washington proposes to make all things American the global standard. Although the actual formulations are of course far more sophisticated, political "spin" is the order of the day in UN forums.

Reform discussions have become largely divorced from today's real world problems. Enlarging the Security Council would not have resolved the major power disagreements over Iraq in 2003. Nor would such reforms bring significantly more pressure to bear on the oppressive governments of Myanmar and Zimbabwe—in fact, most of the proposed changes could well have the opposite effect by reinforcing the distortions of regional loyalties. And while the Responsibility to Protect should surely be more formally endorsed, one should also ask why the already signed, sealed and delivered Convention on Genocide has been the proverbial "scrap of paper" for Darfur. Moreover, it is doubtful that UN reforms now on the table would produce a means to make up the resource deficits for implementing the Millennium Development Goals or pulling countries like the Democratic Republic of the Congo, Haiti or Somalia up by their bootstraps.

None of this is to say that reform is not urgent, only to reiterate that changed behavior of member states is more likely to be the catalyst for reform than the other way around.

Prospects

All other things being equal, the outlook is that the UN will continue to muddle along—achieving a great deal, but somehow unable to approach its true potential. There is little chance of a breakthrough until leadership is found that will impel member states to come to grips with the underlying political, economic and cultural competitions that repeatedly gum up the UN's inner workings. Recent reforms to create the Human Rights Council, split off a logistics department for peacekeeping and set up an office of disarmament, were largely cosmetic, and they will make only marginal differences on the ground.

Much will depend on whether the newly emerging powers—the BRICs and the several others on their economic heels—take more positive roles in UN affairs. So far the signs are not encouraging. Like most member states, these governments have pursued narrowly defined national interests. Nonetheless, as they adjust to their new status, a broadening consultative process with the US and EU could engage these nations more constructively in the full range of UN activities. And that could make a difference.

Reforms and evolutionary change may also come about under pressure from the kaleidoscope of new partnerships that are bringing together civil society, business and governments. These worldwide public policy networks continue to grow, spurred on by globalization and advances in information technology, but governments and UN entities have been slow to fully appreciate and exploit their potential.

When all is said and done, however, real progress toward a more effective UN depends in the first instance on Washington.

The American keystone

Any quantum leap forward by the UN awaits the day when Washington rejoins the fold of governments committed to realizing the vision of the UN Charter. As long as the US remains a disaffected dead weight, the UN cannot generate substantial forward momentum. Nor, for the foreseeable future at least, can any other nation or group of nations establish a truly global entity without the US. While resolutions in the General Assembly may periodically castigate Washington, any attempt to turn the UN into a significant anti-American counterweight would destroy the organization as we know it.

Washington's markedly more conciliatory approach since the election of 2006 is welcome, but it is hardly a new foreign policy. At the UN, Ambassador Khalilzad was quick to win back friends driven off by his acerbic predecessor, but his mission will remain burdened by his bosses' discredited policies and by UN bashers embedded in the Bush Administration woodwork. Washington will necessarily be consumed for Bush's remaining time in office by Iraq and the cauldron that is the Middle East. Actions in other foreign policy areas are unlikely to go beyond tweaks.

Two Washington policy themes have come to the fore that bear on future US relationships with the UN. The first is to be found in calls for active multilateralism and the second, in arguments for greater adherence to American values in foreign policy. The word "multilateralism" still causes some confusion between its common sense meaning of working with others and neocon definitions which gave the term disagreeable overtones of appeasement or agreement for agreement's sake. The EU and Washington have at times adopted the phrase "effective multilateralism," defined by the EU's foreign policy chief, Javier Solana, as "rules with teeth," or the opposite of "feel-good multilateralism." This rather contrived distinction will go unnoticed by most Americans, who have expressed a straightforward desire to repair relations with traditional allies and cast aside the arrogant language of American neocons that still jars from the time of US-European disagreements over the invasion of Iraq.

Support for "American values" will be good ammunition for US presidential candidates. It can be a provocative phrase when presented in the context of Abu Ghraib torture scenes, "extraordinary renditions," eavesdropping on US citizens and Guantanamo interrogations. Shaken by polls that showed the US to have an extraordinarily low standing in the eyes of others around the world, many Americans have called not just for change in specific policies, but also for an overall return to a foreign policy rooted in American traditions of liberty, justice, equality, peace and tolerance. In short, the ideals which Americans drew upon to write the UN Charter.

Going into 2008, it has become popular to promote concepts like favoring diplomacy over military force, getting back in sync with allies, reestablishing US leadership around the globe, and signing on to mainstream international treaties. Although Democratic Party presidential candidates will be the loudest champions of such policies, moderate Republicans lean markedly in this direction. No single book laid out problems with America's unilateralist course better than *Rogue Nation* by Clyde Prestowitz, once a high-level official in the Reagan Administration. Brent Scowcroft, National Security Advisor under George H.W. Bush, and Republican Senator Chuck Hagel have also echoed Democrats in arguing for more principled foreign policies, rooted in western democratic traditions and international cooperation.

Regrettably, however, for progressives who dream of early US actions like supporting the International Criminal Court or acceding to CEDAW, even a greatly strengthened liberal/centrist majority in Congress may not be enough to get the job done. In 2008 and beyond, there will still be bedrock conservatives in the US Senate, and with that body's arcane procedures, opponents can dig in their heels to make ratification extremely difficult for even the most sensible international agreement, as evidenced by the pigeonholing of the Treaty on the Rights of the Child.

Still, White House leadership can make a difference. President George H. W. Bush and his Secretary of State, James Baker, kept Senate conservatives in check to build their successful UN coalition for the Gulf War and to work closely with the Soviet Union's Mikhail Gorbachev on issues such as post-Cold War nuclear disarmament. The lesson is that the next US President will serve the nation well by taking the important international issues to the public and Congress early on in his/her term. Brookings President Strobe Talbot and William Antholis have recently stressed the value of this approach in connection with negotiations on climate change and trade,[78] but the logic applies across the board.

Judging from public opinion surveys and the national elections of 2006, policies to take the world lead on strengthening the UN will have strong popular support.

We believe it is clearly in America's interest to do so and offer the following framework:

Eight policy planks to energize the UN and restore US world standing

1. Make the UN a true cornerstone of American foreign policy.

Strengthening the UN should be a cornerstone of every democracy's foreign policy. American political leaders, neocons excepted, have always extolled UN ideals and the vision of its founders. The US has continued to fund much of the UN's "good works" and selectively exploited American power in the Security Council and Bretton Woods Institutions. But Washington has done little to help realize the full potential of the UN as a universal organization.

To lead in the UN means recommitment to the Charter's goals and actively working for an organization capable of fulfilling the Charter's missions. It means making the kind of pledge, quoted in this book's introduction, that John F. Kennedy voiced at his inauguration: "to strengthen (the UN's) shield of the new and the weak—and to enlarge the area in which its writ may run." JFK's words still capture the essence of today's over-arching issues, namely enlarging the international community's capacity to deal with security threats, and providing compassionate assistance to the less fortunate.

A pro-UN policy declaration by itself will not be enough. Effective leadership in the UN will require presidential engagement to set overall policy and assure priority attention to implementation throughout the Administration. It will also demand the appointment of a truly outstanding American Ambassador—ideally, restoring Cabinet status to the office—and greatly strengthening the corps of diplomatic personnel assigned to multilateral affairs in the State Department, at the US Mission to the UN, and at other major capitals.

2. Work with allies.

On the surface, this is a no-brainer. Everyone, including George W. Bush, is in favor of working more closely with allies. With respect to UN affairs, even in the darkest days of trans-Atlantic feuding there has always been good contact between American diplomats and those of the EU, Japan, Canada, New Zealand and Australia. When this group agrees on objectives, it can swing a lot of weight, and when they don't see eye to eye, the consultative process bridges at least part of the difference or minimizes damage to relations in other areas.

But consultation is a place-holding operation. To energize the UN, Washington needs to drive events with pro-active cooperation through common long term strategies. The Europeans, buoyed by strong popular support back home, will continue to push for enhancing the UN and international law. They will welcome an American shift back to joining in, even if the French or others will from time to time grumble at American domination.

3. Work inside the UN with BRICs and other friends.

Outside the UN, America has constructive relationships with most regional powers: Brazil, India, South Africa, Egypt, Pakistan, India, and others. Inside the UN, these countries all too often work completely at cross purposes with the US on critical items such as electing members to UN bodies and advancing the reform agenda. Hard-nosed diplomacy can change this picture.

America, partnering with Europeans, can do better to enlist the regional powers in common efforts to strengthen the UN. The solution is not simply to threaten retributions or withhold benefits granted in other areas—that rarely works and often boomerangs. It would also be naïve to think that giant steps will follow easily, but assiduous diplomacy can accomplish a great deal, as Ambassador Thomas Pickering demonstrated by achieving repeal of the Zionism-is-racism resolution in 1992. There is no great secret here—finding agreement starts with understanding the needs of the other side, patient bargaining, and willingness to compromise without sacrificing essential interests.

4. Make the Security Council more effective.

A stronger Security Council is in America's interest, and more aggressive US participation can improve its performance, even though member disagreements will at times hamstring the Council. The Council's sweeping and varied agenda overtaxes both the Secretariat support staff and member state missions to the UN. Given the plight of millions around the world, the solution is not to cut back on Council activities, but to make available the resources needed for the tasks at hand. With Charter reform stalled, the US should promote further expansion of consultations and open meetings to enhance the transparency essential for beefing up international support of Council actions.

A new, more forceful US presence should also insist on better use of the Security Council's coordination and oversight powers. The Council for example, should require higher standards and more pro-active performance from its counter-terrorism machinery; it should heed the 2005 Summit call for closer cooperation with the High Commissioner for Human Rights; it should move ahead with measures to reduce trafficking in small arms (hobbled as of mid-2007 by US objections); it should accelerate its important initiative on post-conflict recovery (known as Security Sector Reform); and it should institute more intensive monitoring of Council-mandated missions to preclude the laxity that allowed the oil-for-food and Congo sex abuse scandals to fester.

5. Embrace the rule of law and cooperation on human rights.

Washington loves high-sounding rhetoric, but as we have seen, its policies have directly undercut the international rule of law, except in commercial matters, for a quarter century. The next President should revive America's commitment to international law and strong multilateral institutions. The specific actions needed to put America back on track include a return to accepting the compulsory jurisdiction of the ICJ, finding a formulation that allows the US to support the ICC, and ratifying seminal treaties embraced by all of America's allies: CEDAW, the Law of the Sea, and the Rights of the Child. Down the line, Washington should also withdraw the reservation that emasculated American ratification of the Convention on Genocide.

The new Human Rights Council got off to a dysfunctional start in 2007, but other parts of the UN human rights machinery remain an important force for good, and it is possible to improve the Council itself. The UN's system of independent experts and periodic country reviews should be better exploited to identify violations and increase pressure for change. Governments, in particular democracies, should be held more accountable for their actions in the HRC. Opting out of the HRC as the Bush Administration did has accomplished nothing—opting back in will give America both a forum to make its voice heard and more negotiating opportunities to influence outcomes.

6. Take the lead on disarmament and non-proliferation.

Although stopping Iran's march to nuclear weapons will have to be addressed as an urgent special case, the next US President needs to develop a comprehensive strategy for nuclear arms control, understandable to the public and acceptable to

Congress. Washington should call in all the experts and systematically examine the many good ideas that have been brewing: reenergizing the NPT regime, reviving the CTBT, creating an international nuclear fuel bank, reducing deployed nuclear weapons to zero, safeguarding all nuclear weapons and material, and evaluating America's own nuclear posture, in particular to assess the need for the development of an anti-missile program and a new nuclear warhead.

In other areas, the Bush Administration's refusal to support many arms control activities has held up progress and perplexed America's friends. The promising draft to strengthen the Biological Weapons Convention regime, taken off the table by the US in 2001, should be put back in play. For the Chemical Weapons Convention, steps should be taken to get the four main hold-outs to sign, to accelerate destruction of existing stocks and to beef up the verification regime. Finally, Washington has been a reluctant participant in efforts to curb the use of cluster bombs and land mines and to control trafficking in small arms and light weapons—a fresh look would surely be in America's interests.

7. Get behind the MDGs.

The Millennium Development Goals brought order out of a jumble of programs and priorities. They have broad international support, they are achievable, and achieving them would expand possibilities for more constructive development aid programs in the future. Having endorsed the goals in a general way, Washington should move from its lukewarm support to give them high priority. And, in line with the kind of coordinated approach the US has long advocated, the Millennium Challenge Account should be folded into multilateral programs more directly supporting the MDGs.

Reform of US development assistance programs is past due. America can and should give more. Steps should also be taken to undo the web of ties to US suppliers and shippers that sharply reduces what is ultimately delivered in the field and can defeat the intended purpose of aid programs.

8. Join the consensus to tackle global warming.

It would be superfluous to do more than note here the formidable chorus calling on the Bush Administration to deal forcefully with climate change. The next US Administration seems certain to join the mainstream—doing so will not only refurbish America's image, but will also bring US initiative and technological capabilities to bear more strongly on finding solutions.

◆   ◆   ◆

America's leadership credentials have been greatly diminished in recent years, but its wealth and power remain predominant, and its civil society organizations spearhead positive change on many fronts around the world. The American people aspire to a government that will again be the global leader of international cooperation to secure human rights, promote the rule of law, fight poverty and disease, protect the environment and make the world a more peaceful, safer place. The UN remains a ready and promising vehicle to advance all these goals.

Endnotes

1. Steven Kull, Principal Investigator, *What Kind of Foreign Policy Does the American Public Want*, The PIPA/Knowledge networks Poll, October 20, 2006

2. One of the most articulate and comprehensive presentations of this general view can be found in G. John Ikenberry and Anne-Marie Slaughter, *Forging a World of Liberty under Law: US national Security in the 21st Century*, Final Paper of the Princeton Project on National Security, The Woodrow Wilson School of Public and International Affairs, Princeton University, September 27, 2006

3. Paul Kennedy, *The Parliament of Man*, New York, Random House, 2006

4. Timothy E Wirth, *A Golden Opportunity: The US-UN Relationship*, Testimony before the Committee on Foreign Affairs, US House of Representatives, February 13, 2007

5. Richard Haass, *The Opportunity: America's Moment to Alter History's Course,* New York, Public Affairs, 2005

6. Alison Broinowski and James Wilkinson, *The Third Try: can the UN work?*, Melbourne, Scribe Publications, 2005

7. Rosmary Righter, *Utopia Lost: The United Nations and World Order*, New York, The Twentieth Century Fund Press, 1995

8. Peter J. Spiro, "The New Sovereigntism: American Exceptionalism and Its False Prophets," *Foreign Affairs* Nov/Dec 2000

9. Robert Kagan, *Of Paradise and Power: America and Europe in the New World Order*, New York, A.A. Knopf, 2003

10. NAM, pronounced to rhyme with dam, is the acronym for the Non-Aligned Movement. G-77 is short for Group of 77, so named from the original number of participants when it was started in 1964. The development and current activities of both are discussed later in this chapter.

11. See the G-77 website: www.g77.org

12. Coral Bell, *A World Our of Balance: American Ascendancy and International Politics in the 21st Century*, Sydney, Longueville Books, 2003

13. Abba Eban, "The UN Idea Revisited," *Foreign Affairs*, Vol. 74, September/October 1995

14. Gareth Evans, "The United Nations: Vision, Reality and Reform," address to Australian Fabian Society, Melbourne, 28 September, 2005 (from www.crisisgroup.org)

15. quoted by Richard Gardner, "To Make the World Safe for Interdependence," *UN 30*, New York, United Nations Association-USA, 1976.

16. "World Publics Favor New Powers for the UN," May 9, 2007, report of the Chicago Council on Global Affairs and WorldPublicOpinion.org

17. Rich Morin and Richard Wike, "New UN Chief Heads and Organization that Faces Both Skepticism and Support," Pew Research Center Publications, December 20, 2006, accessed September 29 at www.pewresearch.org

18. Lydia Saad, "United Nations Ratings Remain at Lowest Ebb: Still Americans want UN to contribute to international policy making," Gallup News Service February 06, 2007

19. World Public Opinion.org, "UN Continues to get Positive, though Lower Ratings with World Public," from www.worldpublicopininon.org, accessed September 29, 2007

20. John Gerard Ruggie, *Winning the Peace: America and World Order in the New Era*, New York, Columbia University Press, 1996

21. Samantha Power, "United It Wobbles," *The Washington Post*, January 7, 2007

22. Mark Malloch Brown, "Holmes Lecture: Can the UN be reformed?," annual meeting of the American Council on the UN System, June 7, 2007, from www.globalpolicy.org, accessed September 29, 2007

23. at www.un.org/peace, the Peace and Security pages of the UN website have a wealth of information on all aspects of UN peace operations

24. Dafna Linzer, "Iran Is Judged Ten Years from Nuclear Bomb," *Washington Post*, August 2, 2005, A1

25. The remark was reported on a CBS national TV program. The quote here was taken from a follow-up article: Sheldon Richman, 'Iraqi Sanctions: Were They Worth It?,' *Future of Freedom Foundation,* January 2004, from http://www.globalpolicy.org/security/sanction/iraq1/2004/01sanctionsworth.htm May 28, 2005

26. Paul Collier, *The Bottom Billion: Why the Poorest Countries Are Failing and What Can Be Done About It,* Oxford, Oxford University Press, 2007

27. Charles Foster, "International law: another casualty of the Iraq war?," *Contemporary Review*, August 2003

28. Nagendra Singh, "The UN and the Development of International Law," in *United Nations, Divided World*, Adam Roberts and Benedict Kingsbury Eds, Clarendon Press-Oxford 1993. In the 1928 Kellog-Briand Pact, major powers of the day including Germany, Japan, the US, and the UK renounced war as an instrument of policy, but it was a voluntary declaration with no enforcement provisions—and soon ignored by the fascist signatories.

29. Jane Boulden and Thomas G. Weiss, *Terrorism and the UN,* Bloomington, Indiana University Press, 2004

30. Americans Say US Should Comply with UN Judgment and Change Treatment of Guantanamo Detainees, WorldPublicOpinion.org, November 8, 2007

31. SIPRI—the Stockholm International Peace Research Institute—produces an excellent annual report on military spending.

32. Rosemary Righter, *Utopia Lost: the United Nations and World Order,* The Twentieth Century Fund Press, New York 1995

33. The website of the UN Office at Geneva, www.unog.ch, has official information on the CD and its activities. As of March 2005, the Director-General of UNOG was also the Secretary-General of the CD as well as the Personal Representative of the UN Secretary-General to the CD.

34. For a comprehensive discussion, see Graham Allison, *Nuclear Terrorism: the Ultimate Preventable Catastrophe*, Times Books 2004

35. A number of think tanks have addressed this topic. Views differ—we have relied heavily on material from the Carnegie Endowment for Interna-

tional Peace and its Proliferation News, the Nuclear Control Institute and the Brookings Institution, all headquartered in Washington, DC.

36. For a good overview of the Israeli program see: Warner D. Farr, LTC, U.S. Army, *The Third Temple's Holy of Holies: Israel's Nuclear Weapons*, USAir Force Counterproliferation Center, Air War College, Alabama September 1999

37. For a concise analysis of the national interests motivating today's nuclear powers, see Sverre Lodgaard, *Obstacles to No-First-Use*, a paper presented to Pugwash Meeting No. 279, London, UK, November 15–17, 2002 (http://www.pugwash.org/reports/nw/op2_2/opv2n2_6.htm)

38. George P Shultz, Henry A. Kissinger, William J. Perry and Sam Nunn, "A World Free of Nuclear Weapons," *Wall Street Journal*, January 4, 2007

39. Jessica Tuchman Matthews, "Reinvigorate Nuclear Nonproliferation, *Democracy: A Journal of Ideas*, Issue 6, Fall 2007

40. This Part particularly draws on two Australian studies: Christian Reus-Smit (ed.), "The Challenge of UN Reform", (Keynotes, 05, ANU, RSPAS, Department of International Relations, Canberra: National Library of Australia, 2004); and Gary Klintworth's chapter in Coral Bell (ed.) *The United Nations and Crisis Management: Six Studies* (Canberra Papers on Strategy and Defence, no. 104, ANU, RSPAS, Canberra, 1994). Emeritus Professor Ivan Shearer, a member of the Human Rights Committee 2000–2008, led us to the work on human rights of eminent jurists Philip Alston and Thomas Buergenthal. (see References) Dr Simon Chesterman spoke with us in New York in October 2004: his *You, the People: The United Nations, Transitional Administration, and State-Building* (Oxford: OUP, 2004) and his chapter in Rich and Newman, 2004 take the discussion further.

41. Jeane Kirkpatrick, Ambassador to the UN under Reagan, is George W. Bush's appointee as US Ambassador to the Commission on Human Rights.

42. see www.iciss-ciise.gc.ca

43. The "Charter bodies", set up in 1948, are the Commission on Human Rights (now the Human Rights Council) and the Sub-Commission on the Promotion and Protection of Minorities (the name changed to "of Human Rights" in 1999). The "Treaty bodies", each servicing its match-

ing Convention or Covenant, are the Human Rights Committee (HRC) on civil and political rights, the Committee on the Elimination of Racial Discrimination (CERD), the Committee on Economic and Social and Cultural Rights, the Committee Against Torture, the Committee on the Elimination of Discrimination Against Women (CEDAW), the Committee on the Rights of the Child, and the Committee on Protection of Rights of All Migrant Workers and their Families. The members of all these committees are elected by the UNGA as "independent" experts. Four of the committees can consider direct complaints from individuals about the failure of states to carry out their commitments to the treaties.

44. Hilary Charlesworth, "The United Nations Human Rights System", in Christian Reus-Smit, 2004: 11–17

45. Secret Bush memo, 7 February 2002, paraphased by Seymour Hersh, *Chain of Command: the Road from 9/11 to Abu Ghraib,* New York: Harper Collins, 2004.

46. *Washington Post, SMH,* 29 December 2004: 13. Michael Gawenda, *SMH,* 8 March 2005: 8.

47. "Beijing Betrayed," Report of the Women's Environment and Development Organization, 2005 from www.wedo.org

48. Roberta Cohen's experiences as a human rights monitor inform her 1998 work with Francis M. Deng. Professor Spencer Zifcak has published two essays on Australia's record: *Mr Ruddock Goes to Geneva* (UNSW Press, 2003) and 'Second Opinion: How Australia is undermining the UN', *The Diplomat* (October-November 2004: 18). Australia's human rights performance is also commented on by Anne Bayefsky, *The UN Human Rights Treaty System: Universality at the Crossroads,* http:///www.bayefsky.com

49. All figures from http://www.un.org/millenniumgoals/pdf/mdg2007/pdf

50. David Brown, 'Women being hit hardest by AIDS', *Washington Post, SMH,* 25 November 2004: 11

51. Rachel Mayanja, Statement at the 10th Session of the Regional Conference on Women in Latin America and the Caribbean, Quito, Ecuador, August 6, 2007 accessed at http://www.un.org/womenwatch/osagi/on September 29, 2007

52. *Sydney Morning Herald,* 14 March 2005: 10.

53. Tim Judah's report, 'Uganda: The Secret War' (*NYRB*, vol. LI, no. 14, 23 September 2004: 62–4) together with The UN Foundation, New York, documented the issue in 'Demobilizing Child Soldiers', 2004, as did several Human Rights Watch reports, including *Abused and Abducted: Renewed Conflict in Northern Uganda* (July 2003). International Crisis Group, *Northern Uganda: Understanding and Solving the Conflict*, (April 2004). The UN's Office for the Coordination of Humanitarian Affairs (OCHA) website: www.irinnews.org has updated details.

54. Sharon Bessell, 'The Trafficking of Children through a Human Rights Lens', Canberra: ANU, 2004.

55. Former UN High Commissioner for Refugees, Sadako Ogata, gives a first-hand account in *The Turbulent Decade: Confronting the Refugee Crises of the* 1990s, New York: Norton, 2005. On human rights in Africa, Samantha Power broke new ground with *A Problem from Hell: American Power in an Age of Genocide* (New York: Basic Books, 2002), and 'Bystanders to Genocide: Why the United States Let the Rwandan Tragedy Happen,' (*The Atlantic Monthly*, September 2001), and Samantha Power and Graham Allison (eds.) *Realizing human rights: moving from inspiration to impact*, New York: St Martin's Press, 2000. Australia's refugee policy was accessibly dissected in David Marr and Marian Wilkinson, *Dark Victory* (Sydney: Allen & Unwin, 2003). Indian writer Arundathi Roy gave the 2004 City of Sydney Peace Prize lecture in November 2004: see Peace & The New Corporate Liberation Theology, http://www.arts.usyd.edu.au/centres/cpacs/

56. Human Rights Watch, from www.hrw.org main refugee overview page, accessed October 6, 2007

57. UNHCR, *The State of the World's Refugees: in search of solutions*, Oxford: OUP, 1995

58. Preface, *Masses in Flight: The Global Crisis of Internal Displacement*, Washington: Brookings Institution, 1998

59. Walter Kälin and Dennis McNamara, foreword, Simon Bagshaw and Diane Paul, *Protect or Neglect? Toward a More Effective United Nations Approach to the Protection of Internally Displaced Persons: An Evaluation*, Washington: Brookings-SAIS and United Nations, 2004: vii

60. Roberta Cohen, "'What's So Terrible About Rape?' and Other Attitudes at the United Nations," SAIS Review, Summer/Fall 2000, vol XX no 2: 73–77. Claudia Rosett, "The Real Refugee Scandal", Wall Street Journal, 23 February 2005, www.opinionjournal.Com/forms/print

61. Greg Myre, "Israel Feuds with Agency Set Up to Aid Palestinians," *New York Times* 18 October 2004: A6.

62. Brian Urquhart, "Humanitarianism is Not Enough," *New York Review of Books,* Volume 52, Number 9, 26 May 2005: 26–29.

63. "Indigenous Peoples—Fact Sheet," International Fund for Agricultural Development, Rome, from www.ifad.org accessed October 25, 2007

64. From the vast literature on aid and the IFIs we have particularly drawn on the contrasting opinions of Jeffrey Sachs, William Easterly, Paul Collier, George Monbiot, George Soros, James Wolfensohn, and Keith Suter (see References). Paul Theroux's *Dark Star Safari* (2002) has given us an extra dimension. The UN Development Index and the World Bank's and IMF's annual reports are of course important sources. On the Bank, we have also drawn on Sebastian Mallaby, *The World's Banker : A Story of Failed States, Financial Crises, and the Wealth and Poverty of Nations*, New York: Penguin Press, 2004

65. 'Asian Approaches to Peace and Security and the Role of the United Nations,' Lowy Institute, 1–3 October 2004: 4

66. Susan George and Fabrizio Sabelli, *Faith and Credit: The World Bank's Secular Empire*, Boulder, Westview Press, 1994: 59, 2

67. Progress Towards the Millennium Development Goals, 1990–2005, Goal 1, Statistics Division, UN Department of Economic and Social Affairs, from unstats.un.org/unsd/mi/goals_2005/goal_1.pdf, accessed October 25, 2007

68. F. Bourguignon, and M. Sundberg, "Aid Effectiveness—Opening the Black Box," World Bank paper presented at the American Economics Association annual meeting January 5–7, 2007

69. Oxfam International, *Rigged Rules and Double Standards: Trade, Globalization and the Fight Against Poverty*, Oxford: Oxfam, 2002. Monbiot, 2003: 188

70. http://www.un.org/millenniumgoals/pdf/mdg/2007-pdf

71. Sources on new threats to security include Alan Dupont, *East Asia Imperilled: transnational challenges to* security, New York: Cambridge University Press, 2001; Jared Diamond, *Collapse: How Societies Choose to Fail or Survive*, London: Allen Lane 2004; and Diamond, *Guns, Germs, and Steel: the Fates of Human Societies*, London: Allen Lane 1997); Stephen Mallaby, *The World's Banker: a story of failed states, financial crises, and the wealth and poverty of nations*, New York: Penguin, 2004; Edward Newman and Roland Rich, *The UN Role in promoting democracy: between ideals and reality*, Tokyo: UNU, 2004;and Michael Maren, *The Road to Hell: the Ravaging Effects of Foreign Aid and International Charity*, New York: Free Press, 1997. Articles and broadcasts by Sydney's UN-observer Keith Suter have been useful.

72. Reuben Kyama and Donald G. McNeill, Jr., "Distribution of nets splits malaria fighters," *New York Times,* October 9, 2007

73. WHO Media Center, Fact sheet No. 104, revised March 2007, www.who.int, accessed October 25, 2007

74. WHO Media Center, Fact sheet No. 286, revised January 2007, www.who.int, accessed October 25, 2007

75. United Nations website, Millennium Development Goals Report, 2007

76. Edward Newman and Roland Rich, *The UN Role in promoting democracy: between ideals and reality*, Tokyo: UNU, 2004

77. Transparency International, *Australian* August 23, 2004: 17

78. See the website www.opportunity08.org set up by the Brookings Institution in partnership with ABC News to discuss issues in connection with the the 2008 presidential election.

Acronyms

ABC	Australian Broadcasting Corporation
ABM	Anti-Ballistic Missile (Treaty)
AGPS	Australian Government Publishing Service
AIDS	Acquired Immune Deficiency Syndrome
ASEAN	Association of Southeast Asian Nations
AU	African Union
BBC	British Broadcasting Commission
CEDAW	International Convention on the Elimination of All Forms of Discrimination Against Women (UN)
CIA	Central Intelligence Agency (US)
CPA	Coalition Provisional Authority (Iraq)
CRC	International Convention on the Rights of the Child (UN)
CT	International Convention Against Torture
CTBT	Comprehensive Test Ban Treaty
DDR	Dismantle, demobilize, reintegrate
DPA	Department of Peacekeeping Affairs (UN)
DPKO	Department of Peacekeeping Operations (UN)
ECOSOC	Economic and Social Council (UN)
G7, G8	Group of Seven (industrialized countries) Eight (with Russia)
GDP	Gross Domestic Product
GNI	Gross National Income
GNP	Gross National Product
HIV	Human Immune-deficiency Virus

HLP	High Level Panel (UN)
HRC	Human Rights Council (UN)
IAEA	International Atomic Energy Agency (UN)
IASC	Interagency Standing Committee (UN and non-UN)
IBRD	International Bank for Reconstruction and Development
ICC	International Criminal Court (UN)
ICCPR	International Covenant on Civil and Political Rights (UN)
ICISS	International Commission on Intervention and State Sovereignty
ICG	International Crisis Group
ICJ	International Court of Justice (UN)
IDD	Iodine Deficiency Disease
IDP	Internally Displaced Person
IFAD	International Fund for Agricultural Development (UN)
IFC	International Finance Corporation
IFI	International Financial Institution(s)
IFRC	International Federation of Red Cross and Red Crescent Societies
ILC	International Law Commission
ILO	International Labor Organization
IRRI	International Rice Research Institute
INTERFET	International Force for East Timor
MDG	Millennium Development Goals
MONUC	UN Military Mission in the Democratic Republic of the Congo
NATO	North Atlantic Treaty Organization
NGO	Non-Governmental Organization
NYRB	*New York Review of Books*
NYT	*New York Times*
OAU	Organization of African Unity
OCHA	Office of the Coordinator of Humanitarian Affairs (UN)

ODA	Overseas Development Assistance
OFF	Oil for Food (UN program)
OXFAM	Oxford Committee for Famine Relief
P5 or **Perm-5**	Permanent Five (members of UNSC)
PKO	Peacekeeping Operation (UN)
PSI	Preventive Security Initiative
R2P	Responsibility to Protect
SC	Security Council (UN)
SMH	*Sydney Morning Herald*
SPLA	Sudanese People's Liberation Army
UN	United Nations
UNAMA	UN Mission in Afghanistan
UNAMI	UN Assistance Mission in Iraq
UNMIS	UN Mission in Sudan
UNCTAD	UN Committee on Trade, Aid, and Development
UNDP	UN Development Program
UNEP	UN Environment Program
UNESCO	UN Educational, Scientific, and Cultural Commission
UNGA	UN General Assembly
UNHCHR	UN High Commissioner for Human Rights
UNHCR	UN High Commission (Commissioner) for Refugees
UNHRC	UN Human Rights Commission
UNICEF	UN Children's Fund
UNIDO	UN Industrial Development Organization
UNMISET	UN Mission in East Timor
UNMOVIC	UN Observation and Verification Mission in Cambodia
UNOMB	UN Observation Mission in Bougainville
UNODC	UN Office on Drugs and Crime

UNRWA	UN Relief and Works Agency
UNSC	UN Security Council
UNSCOM	UN Special Commission (Iraq)
UNTAET	UN Transitional Administration in East Timor
UNTAG	UN Transitional Assistance Group (Namibia)
UNU	UN University
WEF	World Economic Forum
WFP	World Food Program
WMD	Weapons of Mass Destruction
WSF	World Social Forum

About the Authors

M. James Wilkinson served as Deputy US Representative on the Security Council with the rank of Ambassador. Since retiring from his career in the American Foreign Service, he has been active in civic organizations and writing on international affairs.

Dr Alison Broinowski, formerly an Australian diplomat at the United Nations, teaches graduate students at Macquarie University and heads a research project on Asian/Australian fiction at the University of Wollongong. Her latest book is *Allied and Addicted* (2007).

Index

978-0-595-48025-8
0-595-48025-X

www.ingramcontent.com/pod-product-compliance
Lightning Source LLC
Chambersburg PA
CBHW030322290526
45785CB00001B/474